ORCHIDS
PLANT CARE
GUIDE

THE COMPLETE RESOURCE FOR GROWING, NURTURING,
AND CULTIVATING THE WORLD'S MOST EXOTIC BLOOMS
FROM BEGINNER TO EXPERT

JANE POTTS

© COPYRIGHT

DISCLAIMER

Table Of CONTENTS

1 Introduction to Orchids

2 Getting Started

3 Orchid Care Fundamentals

4 Advanced Orchid Care

5 Specific Orchid Care

6 Troubleshooting and Common Issues

7 Advanced Techniques and Projects

Conclusion

Introduction to Orchids

Orchids Plant Care Guide is a comprehensive guide for orchid enthusiasts of all skill levels. Whether you're just starting to learn about orchids or are an expert cultivator, this book will take you step-by-step through the fascinating world of orchids. Covering a wide array of themes required for successful orchid development, the book presents them in a straightforward and logical approach.

Starting with the basics, it dives into the historical and cultural significance of orchids, providing a rich background for their attractiveness and popularity. Next, the book moves on to the meat of the matter, providing in-depth instructions on how to create the ideal growing conditions, how to choose the right species, and how to make sense of potting soil. As readers proceed, they will find thorough sections on the essential principles of orchid care, including lighting, watering, and fertilization.

For individuals wishing to enhance their expertise, the book covers advanced care procedures, pest and disease management, and propagation strategies. Specific chapters are dedicated to popular orchid variations so that gardeners can adapt to the individual needs of diverse species. Troubleshooting advice and advanced projects further expand the reader's experience, helping them to handle typical issues and start on inventive orchid-growing activities.

Purpose

The major objective of this book is to serve as an all-encompassing resource for orchid growers at every point of their journey. Here's a detailed look at the specific objectives:

1. Educate Beginners: - The book seeks to demystify the world of orchids for beginners by breaking down difficult knowledge into easy and intelligible content. It includes step-by-step guidance on everything from picking the proper orchid to setting up a growing environment and basic maintenance procedures.

2. Expand Knowledge: - For those with some expertise, the book offers deeper insights into the intricacies of orchid care. This includes advanced fertilization procedures, subtle lighting requirements, and temperature management, enabling intermediate growers to enhance their skills.

- Expert Guidance: - For seasoned orchid enthusiasts, the book serves as a guide for sophisticated cultivation procedures, including hybridization and producing new orchid kinds. It also includes new ideas like building an orchid terrarium or greenhouse, stretching the limitations of traditional orchid growing.

- Troubleshooting and Problem Solving: - Recognizing that orchid growing can bring several obstacles, the book includes thorough troubleshooting chapters. These sections are meant to assist growers in recognizing and treating common problems, ensuring their orchids remain healthy and vibrant.

- Inspire innovation: - The book encourages innovation and experimentation among gardeners. Presenting advanced techniques and project ideas stimulates readers to explore new ways of appreciating and showcasing their orchids.

- Resource Compilation: - The appendices offer a wonderful collection of words and further reading resources, making this book not just a guide but a beginning point for continued learning and inquiry in the world of orchids.

- Overall, "Orchids Plant Care Guide" is created to be the essential handbook for orchid growers. Its thorough approach ensures that the book remains a vital resource, offering practical information, advanced techniques, and inspirational ideas for anybody interested in orchids.

Chapter One
What are Orchids?

Orchids are among the most diverse and extensive families of flowering plants, belonging to the Orchidaceae family. This family is one of the largest in the plant kingdom, with about 25,000 species and more than 100,000 hybrids. Orchids can be found in a variety of settings across the globe, from tropical rainforests to deserts, showing a stunning range of forms, colors, and sizes.

Botanical Characteristics

Orchids are recognized for their complex and extremely specialized blossoms, which have evolved unique processes for pollination. The key botanical traits that identify orchids include:

- Bilateral Symmetry: Orchid blossoms are bilaterally symmetrical, meaning they may be separated into mirror-image halves along a single plane. This trait is known as zygomorphy.

- Labellum (Lip): One of the three petals of an orchid flower is generally transformed into a labellum or lip. This lip is frequently bigger and more complex than the other petals and serves to attract and guide pollinators.

- Column: Orchids feature a peculiar reproductive structure called the column, which is a fusion of the male (stamens) and female (pistil) components of the flower. The column often aids the transport of pollen by visiting pollinators.

- Pollinia: Unlike many other flowers that generate loose pollen, orchids produce pollen in compact masses known as pollinia. These pollinia are normally transported as an entire unit during pollination.
- Resupination: Many orchid blooms undergo a process called resupination, where the flower bends 180 degrees during development, putting the labellum at the bottom to better allow pollination.

Growth Habits

Orchids have a range of growth behaviors, which can be broadly divided into three types:

1. Epiphytic Orchids: These orchids grow on other plants, mainly trees, but are not parasitic. They anchor themselves to the host plant using aerial roots, which also take moisture and nutrients from the air and rain. Examples include the popular Phalaenopsis (moth orchids) and Vanda orchids.
2. Terrestrial Orchids: These orchids grow in the ground, with their roots spreading into the earth. They generally thrive in forest floors or meadows. Notable terrestrial orchids include the Cymbidium and Bletilla species.
3. Lithophytic Orchids: These orchids grow on rocks and commonly inhabit cliff walls or rocky outcrops. They anchor themselves in crevices where organic material accumulates. Examples include various species of the Laelia and Paphiopedilum genera.

Ecological Adaptations

Orchids have evolved several adaptations to live in a wide range of settings. These adaptations include:

- Mycorrhizal Associations: Many orchids have symbiotic connections with mycorrhizal fungi, which assist plants to absorb nutrients from the soil, especially during the seedling stage.

- Specialized Pollination Mechanisms: Orchids exhibit a range of pollination techniques, typically involving intricate relationships with specific pollinators such as bees, butterflies, moths, birds, and even some mammals. Some orchids replicate the appearance or perfume of female insects to attract male pollinators.
- Water Storage: In settings where water is scarce, such as on tree branches or rocky surfaces, some orchids have evolved to retain water in their thicker stems, leaves, or pseudobulbs.

Diversity and Classification

The diversity of orchids is tremendous, and they are categorized into various subfamilies, tribes, and genera. Some of the most well-known genera include:

1. Phalaenopsis: Known as moth orchids, these are among the most popular and extensively cultivated orchids due to their stunning, long-lasting blossoms and relative ease of maintenance.
2. Cattleya: Often referred to as the "queen of orchids," Cattleyas are prized for their big, fragrant, and colorful flowers.
3. Dendrobium: This varied genus comprises species with a wide diversity of growth patterns and flower shapes, many of which are popular in cultivation.
4. Oncidium: Known as "dancing lady" orchids, Oncidiums are recognized by their bright, generally yellow blossoms with elaborate patterns.
5. Paphiopedilum: Commonly known as slipper orchids, these are recognized by their peculiar pouch-like labellum, which functions as a trap for pollinators.

Orchids are a monument to the remarkable diversity and adaptability of the plant kingdom.

Chapter 2

History and Cultural Significance of Orchids

Ancient Civilizations and Early Uses

In In ancient China, orchids were highly appreciated not just for their scent and therapeutic capabilities. Confucius, the ancient Chinese philosopher, complimented orchids for their delicate and exquisite aroma, likening the plant to virtuous gentlemen. Traditional Chinese medicine exploited orchid roots and blooms for their alleged health benefits, including treating lung disorders and stimulating the immune system.

In ancient Greece and Rome, orchids were connected with fertility and vitality. The name "orchid" is derived from the Greek word "orchis," which means testicle, a reference to the shape of the plant's tubers. Greek women believed that consuming particular orchid roots may change the sex of their pregnant offspring.

The Aztecs of Mesoamerica held the vanilla orchid in great respect. They used the vanilla bean, obtained from the orchid species Vanilla planifolia, to flavor their chocolate drinks. Vanilla was also utilized as a tribute to the gods and in other rituals.

Orchidelirium and Victorian Fascination

The interest in orchids reached a fever pitch during the Victorian era in the 19th century, a period frequently referred to as "Orchidelirium." Wealthy Europeans, fascinated by the exotic beauty of orchids, supported risky voyages to tropical regions in quest of rare and unusual species. These explorers risked great conditions and hazards, including disease and dangerous locales, to bring back valued specimens.

Orchids became prestige symbols among the Victorian elite, and orchid collecting grew into a competitive and occasionally cutthroat hobby. Greenhouses were developed to produce these exotic plants, and the need for new types encouraged the development of hybridization procedures. This era saw the foundation of big orchid nurseries and the creation of several hybrid types that are still popular today.

Modern Significance

In contemporary times, orchids continue to be icons of luxury and elegance. They are popular in flower arrangements, wedding bouquets, and potted plants. Orchids are also celebrated in art and literature, symbolizing love, beauty, and sophistication.

In various Asian cultures, orchids are connected with prosperity, purity, and perfection. They are often used in traditional festivals and religious events. In Japan, orchids represent refinement and humility, whereas in Thailand, they are considered emblems of fertility and good fortune.

The commercial cultivation of orchids has become a huge industry, with millions of plants being grown and sold globally each year. Advances in cultivation techniques and biotechnology have made it possible to cultivate orchids on a big scale, making them more accessible to enthusiasts and collectors.

Chapter 3
Types of Orchids (species, hybrids, terrestrial, epiphytic)

Species Orchids

Species orchids are those that occur natively in the wild. These orchids have developed over millions of years, adapting to their habitats and creating distinct features. Species orchids are often treasured by collectors for their natural beauty and diversity. **Some well-known species of orchids include:**

- Phalaenopsis: Known as moth orchids, these are among the most popular and extensively cultivated species due to their stunning, long-lasting blossoms and ease of maintenance.
- Cattleya: Often referred to as the "queen of orchids," Cattleyas are noted for their big, fragrant, and colorful flowers.
- Dendrobium: This varied genus comprises species with a wide diversity of growth patterns and flower shapes, many of which are popular in cultivation.
- Paphiopedilum: Commonly known as slipper orchids, these are recognized by their peculiar pouch-like labellum, which functions as a trap for pollinators.
- Vanda: Known for their brilliant, big flowers and frequent flowering, Vanda orchids require high humidity and plenty of sunshine.

Species orchids are sometimes more complex to grow than hybrids because they have distinct environmental needs that must be met to survive.

Hybrid Orchids

Hybrid orchids are formed by cross-breeding several species or genera to produce new variations. These hybrids generally combine attractive qualities from both parent plants, such as unusual flower colors, forms, and growth behaviors. Hybrids can be more durable and easier to grow than species orchids, making them suitable for novices.

Some common hybrid orchids include:

- Phalaenopsis Hybrids: These hybrids are noted for their varied colors and patterns, including spots, stripes, and multi-colored blooms. They are easy to grow and bloom profusely.
- Cattleya Hybrids: Hybridization has developed Cattleyas with an assortment of colors and perfumes, extending their blooming times and making them more adaptable to varied growing situations.
- Dendrobium Hybrids: These hybrids are bred for their gorgeous flowers and robust growth, frequently producing numerous blooms on a single stem.
- Oncidium Hybrids: Known as "dancing lady" orchids, these hybrids have elaborate, vividly colored blossoms and are reasonably easy to care for.

Hybridization has broadened the number of orchids available to farmers, providing more alternatives for anyone wishing to nurture these lovely plants.

Terrestrial Orchids

Terrestrial orchids grow on the earth, with their roots spreading into the soil. They are typically found in forest floors, meadows, and other terrestrial settings. Terrestrial orchids sometimes require well-draining soil and specialized soil amendments to grow. Some prominent terrestrial orchids include:

- Cymbidium: Known for their high, arching flower spikes and persistent blooms, Cymbidiums are popular in floral presentations and as potted plants.

- Bletilla: Also known as Chinese ground orchids, Bletillas are resilient and can be cultivated in garden beds or containers. They produce stunning pink or white flowers.

- Pterostylis: Commonly referred to as greenhood orchids, these plants have unusual hooded blossoms and are native to Australia and New Zealand.

Terrestrial orchids can be cultivated in garden settings or pots, provided they have well-draining soil and sufficient light conditions.

Epiphytic Orchids

Epiphytic orchids grow on other plants, generally trees, although they are not parasitic. Instead, they anchor themselves to the host plant using aerial roots, which also take moisture and nutrients from the air and rain. Epiphytic orchids are typically found in tropical rainforests, where they grow in the damp, shady canopy. Some well-known epiphytic orchids include:

- Phalaenopsis: These orchids are among the easiest to grow and are widely popular for their long-lasting, exquisite blooms.
- Vanda: Vanda orchids are noted for their huge, colorful blossoms and demand high humidity and bright light to thrive.
- Dendrobium: Many species of Dendrobium are epiphytic, producing magnificent flower clusters and demanding well-ventilated circumstances.
- Oncidium: Often referred to as "dancing lady" orchids, Oncidiums feature vivid, complex blossoms and need intermediate to warm conditions.

Epiphytic orchids can be cultivated in baskets, mounted on slabs of bark or wood, or in pots with a well-draining medium that simulates their native habitat, such as bark or sphagnum moss.

Lithophytic Orchids

L Lithophytic orchids grow on rocks and are adaptable to settings with minimal soil. They often grow in nooks where organic material gathers. Examples include various species of the Laelia and Paphiopedilum genera. Lithophytic orchids require excellent drainage and conditions that emulate their rocky environments.

Getting Started

❧

Chapter 4
Setting Up Your Orchid Growing Space

Orchids have certain needs in terms of light, temperature, humidity, and air circulation, and setting up your growing area to fulfill these requirements will considerably boost your chances of success.

Understanding Orchid Needs

Before going into the mechanics of setting up your growing environment, it's necessary to understand the fundamental needs of orchids. Orchids thrive in settings that closely mimic their natural habitats.

Consider:

- **Light:**

Orchids need appropriate light to photosynthesize and produce energy for growth and flowering. Different orchid species have varying light requirements, ranging from low to high.

- **Temperature:**

Orchids are sensitive to temperature swings and generally fall into three categories: cool-growing, intermediate-growing, and warm-growing. Each category has its ideal temperature range.

1. Humidity: Most orchids prefer high humidity levels, often between 50% and 80%. Proper humidity helps avoid dehydration and encourages healthy growth.
2. Air Circulation: Good air circulation is crucial for preventing fungal and bacterial infections and ensuring even temperature and humidity distribution.
3. Watering and Drainage: Orchids require well-draining media and careful watering methods to avoid root rot.

Choosing a Location

The first step in setting up your orchid growing room is finding an acceptable site. Depending on the size of your collection and the varieties of orchids you grow, you can pick a windowsill, a dedicated room, or a greenhouse.

- **Windowsill Growing:**

For tiny collections, a windowsill might be an ideal growing place. Choose a window that receives the correct quantity of light for your orchids. South-facing windows are great for high-light orchids like Cattleyas and Vandas, while east or west-facing windows can support medium-light orchids like Oncidiums and Dendrobiums. North-facing windows are good for low-light orchids like Phalaenopsis.

- **Dedicated Room:**

If you have a larger collection, allocating a full room to your orchids can allow more control over environmental conditions. A spare bedroom, sunroom, or basement can be turned into a thriving orchid refuge. Invest in grow lights to augment natural light and use humidifiers and fans to ensure proper humidity and air circulation.

- **Greenhouse:**

For dedicated orchid fans, a greenhouse offers the ultimate growing environment. Greenhouses provide optimum control over light, temperature, humidity, and air circulation, allowing you to cultivate a wide range of orchids. Choose a greenhouse with adjustable ventilation, shading systems, and heating/cooling choices to accommodate diverse orchid species.

Setting Up Lighting

Proper lighting is vital for orchid growth and blooming. Depending on your chosen location, you may need to complement natural light with artificial illumination.

- Natural Light:

Evaluate the natural light in your growing space. Orchids require varying light intensity, measured in foot-candles:

1. Low light (1,000–1,500 foot-candles): Suitable for Phalaenopsis and Paphiopedilum.
2. Medium light (1,500–3,000 foot-candles): Ideal for Oncidium and Dendrobium.
3. Highlight (3,000–5,000 foot candles): Needed for Cattleya and Vanda.

Use sheer drapes or shade cloth to disperse bright sunlight and prevent leaf burn. Rotate your orchids occasionally to provide even light exposure.

- **Artificial Light:**

If natural light is insufficient, utilize grow lights to provide the appropriate light intensity and duration. LED grow lights are energy-efficient and adaptable to emit specific light spectrums that orchids need. Position the lights 6–12 inches above the plants and alter the time according to the orchids' requirements, often 12–16 hours each day.

Managing Temperature

Orchids have various temperature preferences. Monitor and maintain the optimal temperature range for your orchid species:

- Cool-growing orchids: (50–70°F/10–21°C) include Masdevallia and Cymbidium.
- Intermediate-growing orchids: (55–75°F/13–24°C) include Cattleya and Miltonia.
- Warm-growing orchids: (60–85°F/16–29°C) include Phalaenopsis and Vanda.

Use thermostats to regulate heating and cooling devices. In greenhouses, automated devices can help maintain regular temperatures. In interior installations, space heaters, air conditioners, and fans can be utilized to moderate temperature changes.

Controlling Humidity

Most orchids thrive in high humidity, between 50% and 80%. To maintain ideal humidity levels:

- - Humidifiers: Use humidifiers to improve humidity in indoor growing environments, especially during dry winter months.
- Humidity Trays: Place orchids on trays filled with pebbles and water. As the water evaporates, it raises the surrounding humidity.
- Misting: Regularly mist your orchids to offer additional moisture. Avoid sprinkling in the evening to prevent fungal development.

Greenhouse Humidity: In greenhouses, automated misting systems or evaporative coolers can help maintain ideal humidity levels.

Ensuring Air Circulation

Good air circulation minimizes fungal and bacterial infections and maintains an even distribution of temperature and humidity. To promote air circulation:

- Fans: Use oscillating fans to produce mild air circulation around your orchids. Position the fans to avoid direct airflow on the plants.
- Ventilation: In greenhouses, ensure sufficient ventilation with adjustable vents and exhaust fans to minimize heat and humidity buildup.

Watering and Drainage

Proper watering is crucial for orchid health. Overwatering and inadequate drainage are common causes of root rot. Follow these guidelines:

- Watering Frequency: Water orchids when the growing medium is nearly dry. The frequency depends on the orchid species, potting media, and environmental circumstances.
- Water Quality: Use rainwater, distilled water, or reverse osmosis water to avoid mineral buildup. If using tap water, let it sit overnight to let chlorine evaporate.
- Drainage: Ensure pots have drainage holes. Use well-draining potting material such as bark, sphagnum moss, or a mix of both to offer aeration and prevent waterlogging.

Potting and Mounting Orchids

Choosing the correct container and potting material is vital for orchid health. Orchids can be grown in pots or mounted on various substrates.

POTTING:

1. Plastic Pots: Retain moisture longer and are lightweight. Suitable for most orchids, especially those that prefer more steady hydration.
2. Clay Pots: Provide improved aeration and stability. Ideal for orchids that prefer drier conditions, such as Cattleyas and Dendrobiums.
3. Orchid Baskets: Allow great air circulation and drainage. Suitable for epiphytic orchids like Vandas and some Dendrobiums.

MOUNTING:

1. Mounting on Bark or Wood: Epiphytic orchids can be mounted on slabs of bark, cork, or driftwood to replicate their native environment. Ensure the mounting material is free of chemicals and bugs.
2. Securing the Plant: Use fishing line, twine, or nylon stockings to tie the orchid to the mount. Over time, the orchid will establish itself by sprouting roots into the mounting medium.

Chapter 5
Choosing the Right Orchid for You (beginner-friendly species)

With the large variety of species and hybrids available, it's crucial to start with those that are known for their durability, ease of care, and adaptability.

Phalaenopsis (Moth Orchid)

Phalaenopsis, also known as the moth orchid, is one of the most popular and widely cultivated orchids due to its exquisite and long-lasting flowers. These orchids are characterized by their enormous, flat flowers that mimic moths in flight, with hues ranging from immaculate white to brilliant pinks, purples, and yellows. Phalaenopsis orchids are particularly preferred by beginners due to their forgiving character. They grow in regular domestic conditions, requiring moderate light and consistent temperatures between 65-75°F (18-24°C). These orchids like a potting material that allows their roots to breathe, such as bark or sphagnum moss, and should be watered thoroughly when the medium feels dry, usually every 7-10 days.

Dendrobium

Dendrobium orchids offer a varied range of shapes and sizes, with varieties that produce towering canes adorned with many flowers. These orchids are recognized for their dramatic look, with flowers that can vary significantly in color and form.

For beginners, Dendrobium orchids are a good choice due to their resilience and versatility. They can handle a range of temperatures, from mild to warm, and flourish in bright, filtered light. Dendrobiums require regular watering during their growing season, with the potting media allowed to dry slightly between waterings. During their winter dormancy, water should be lowered. These orchids benefit from a well-draining potting mix and enjoy high humidity levels, around 50-70%.

Cattleya

Cattleya orchids, frequently referred to as the "Queen of Orchids," are known for their big, beautiful, and fragrant blooms. Historically popular for corsages, Cattleyas come in a wide range

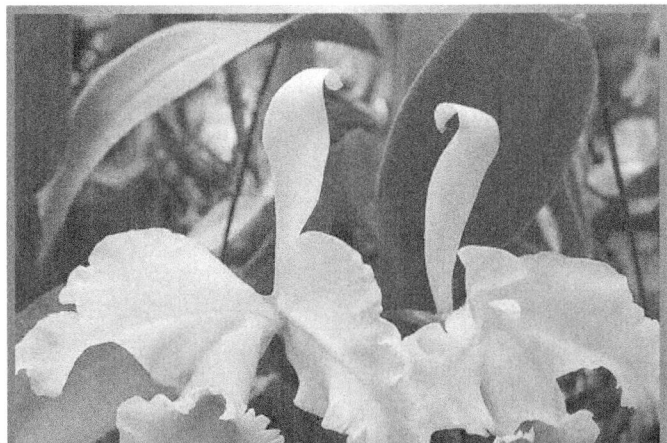

of colors, from vivid purples and pinks to delicate whites and yellows. While significantly more demanding than Phalaenopsis and Dendrobium, Cattleyas are still achievable for beginners who are ready for a bit of a challenge. These orchids demand strong light, including some direct sunshine, and flourish in warm to intermediate temperatures, with nighttime temperatures around 60-70°F (16-21°C) and daytime temperatures of 70-85°F (21-29°C). Cattleyas prefer a potting medium that dries out between waterings, such as coarse bark. They should be watered thoroughly and then let to dry out, typically every 7-10 days.

Oncidium (Dancing Lady Orchid)

Oncidium orchids, known as dancing lady orchids, are instantly identified by their sprays of petite, complex blossoms that often resemble dancing figures. These orchids are available in numerous colors, mostly yellow and brown, and may provide a spectacular display when in full bloom.

Oncidiums are reasonably easy to manage and are recognized for their prolific blooming. They adapt well to a range of growth situations, making them perfect for novices. Oncidiums prefer strong, filtered light and intermediate to warm temperatures, around 55-75°F (13-24°C).

Paphiopedilum (Lady's Slipper Orchid)

Paphiopedilum orchids, also known as lady's slipper orchids, are renowned for their unusual, pouch-like flowers and frequently have stunning, mottled foliage. These orchids are native to forest floors and shaded areas, which determines their care requirements.

Lady's slipper orchids are particularly well-suited for beginners because they flourish in lower light levels, making them perfect for indoor gardening. They enjoy cool to intermediate temperatures, ranging from 60-75°F (16-24°C). The potting material should remain consistently moist, thus they should be watered every 5-7 days. Using a potting mix that holds moisture yet allows proper drainage, such as a blend of bark, perlite, and peat moss, is crucial. Regular fertilizing every two weeks during the growing season will support healthy growth and brilliant flowers.

Miltonia (Pansy Orchid)

Miltonia orchids, known as pansy orchids, are admired for their cheery, pansy-like blossoms that come in a spectrum of vibrant colors. They are also noted for their lovely smell, which can fill a room with a sweet scent.

Miltonias are a wonderful choice for novices because they are reasonably straightforward to care for and thrive in regular indoor circumstances. These orchids prefer bright, indirect light and intermediate temperatures, around 60-75°F (16-24°C). The potting media should be kept moist but not saturated, requiring watering every 5-7 days. A mix of bark and sphagnum moss works nicely for Miltonias.

Brassavola

Brassavola orchids are recognized for their stunning, star-shaped blossoms and their powerful, lemony aroma that becomes more noticeable in the evening. These orchids are relatively easy to grow and are highly tolerant of a range of environments.

Brassavolas are well-suited for novices due to their sturdy nature and uncomplicated care requirements. They thrive in bright light, including some direct sunshine, and enjoy mild to intermediate temperatures, around 65-85°F (18-29°C). Brassavolas should be cultivated in a well-draining potting medium, such as coarse bark or a mix of bark and perlite.

Chapter 6
Understanding Orchid Potting Media and Repotting

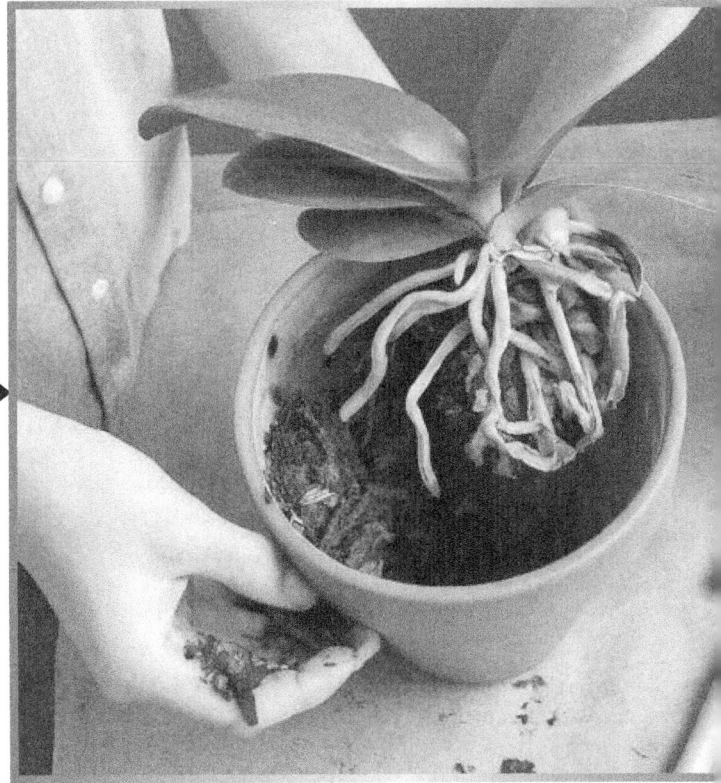

Orchids are unusual in their growing habits and requirements, notably different from normal houseplants. By mastering these crucial features, you can ensure your orchids survive and produce their magnificent flowers.

Orchid Potting Media

Unlike regular soil-based plants, orchids generally require specialized potting media that provide optimum aeration and drainage. The proper potting medium can vary based on the orchid species and the growing conditions. **Here are some of the most often-used orchid potting media:**

- **Bark**

Types of Bark:
1. Fir Bark: The most popular type, noted for its durability and availability.
2. Pine Bark: Often used in blends, it provides good aeration and drainage.
3. Cork Bark: Less common, but offers great drainage and is lightweight.

Benefits:
1. Excellent aeration and drainage.
2. Mimics the natural growing circumstances of epiphytic orchids.
3. Available in various sizes to suit different orchid species.

Drawbacks:
1. Breaks down with time, necessitating regular replacement.
2. Can hold too much moisture if not well-drained.

- **Sphagnum Moss**

Benefits:

1. High moisture retention, making it suitable for orchids that require constantly wet conditions.
2. Provides good aeration despite its moisture-holding capacity.
3. Lightweight and simple to handle.

Drawbacks:

1. Can disintegrate quickly, leading to a compacted medium that impedes root aeration.
2. Requires careful watering to avoid overwatering and root rot.

- **Coconut Husk**

Forms:

1. Chunks: Provide appropriate aeration and drainage.
2. Fiber: Retains more moisture, perfect for orchids demanding continuous humidity.
3. Chips: A balance between chunks and fiber, enabling moderate moisture retention and aeration.

Benefits:

1. Long-lasting compared to bark and sphagnum moss.
2. Sustainable and renewable resources.
3. Good balance of moisture retention and aeration.

Drawbacks:

1. Can retain salts from the manufacturing process, necessitating thorough rinsing before use.
2. May hold too much moisture if not properly controlled.

- **Perlite and Vermiculite**

Perlite:

1. Lightweight volcanic glass that provides great aeration.
2. Often blended with other media to promote drainage.

Vermiculite:

1. Lightweight, absorbent mineral that retains moisture.
2. Used to promote water retention in potting mixtures.

Benefits:

1. Improves the structure of potting mixes by promoting aeration and moisture retention.
2. Non-decomposing, giving a stable environment for roots.

Drawbacks:

1. They are not generally used alone, as they lack the framework needed to support orchids.
2. Can float to the surface when watering, requiring regular correction.

- **Rock Wool**

Benefits:

1. Provides great aeration and moisture retention.
2. Sterile and inert, lowering the danger of sickness.

Drawbacks:

1. Can be difficult to handle and may irritate the skin.
2. Requires careful maintenance to avoid overwatering.

- **Charcoal**

Benefits:

1. Absorbs pollutants and odors, keeping the potting medium fresh.

2. Provides optimum aeration and drainage.

Drawbacks:

1. Can be tough to locate in proper sizes.
2. Does not retain much moisture, requiring careful watering control.

- **Clay Pellets (LECA)**

Benefits:

1. Provides great aeration and drainage.
2. Inert and long-lasting, not breaking down over time.
3. Suitable for semi-hydroponic growing methods.

Drawbacks:

1. Can be hefty, especially for larger pots.
2. Requires particular watering procedures to ensure stable moisture levels.

Selecting the Right Potting Medium

Choosing the correct potting medium for your orchids depends on the individual needs of the orchid species, your growth environment, and your watering habits. Here are some general guidelines:

- Epiphytic Orchids (e.g., Phalaenopsis, Cattleya): Prefer a medium that gives excellent aeration, such as bark or a mix of bark and perlite.
- Terrestrial Orchids (e.g., Paphiopedilum, Cymbidium): Benefit from a medium that holds more moisture, such as a mix of sphagnum moss, perlite, and bark.
- Moisture-Loving Orchids (e.g., Miltonia, Masdevallia): Thrive on a medium that holds moisture effectively, including sphagnum moss or a blend of coconut fiber and perlite.

- Semi-Hydroponic Growing: Requires media that provide regular moisture levels without waterlogging, such as clay pellets (LECA).

Repotting Orchids

Repotting is a crucial component of orchid care, necessary to renew the potting material, accommodate expanding roots, and preserve plant health. Understanding when and how to repot your orchids is vital for their well-being.

When to Repot

Orchids should be repotted under the following conditions:

1. Overgrown Roots: When roots outgrow the pot and begin circling or growing out of the container.
2. Decomposed media: When the potting media breaks down and compacts, decreasing aeration and drainage.
3. Stalled Growth: When the orchid shows evidence of delayed growth or diminished flowering, signaling the need for fresh medium and extra room.
4. Pests or Disease: When there are symptoms of pest infestations or disease in the potting media.

How to Report

Materials Needed:

1. Fresh potting medium suitable for your orchid species.
2. Sterilized pruning shears or scissors.
3. A fresh pot (or disinfected old pot) with enough drainage holes.
4. A work area with ample space to handle the orchid.

Steps:

- **Preparation:**

Water the orchid thoroughly a day before repotting to make the roots more pliable and simpler to handle.

- Prepare the new potting media by soaking it if necessary (e.g., the bark should be soaked to ensure it retains moisture initially).

- **Removing the Orchid:**

Gently remove the orchid from its present pot. If the roots are trapped, gradually pry them free without hurting them.

- Shake off or rinse away old potting medium from the roots.

- **Inspecting and Trimming:**

Inspect the roots for any signs of decay or injury. Healthy roots are solid and white or green.

- Trim away any dead, mushy, or discolored roots with sanitized shears.

- **Positioning the Orchid:**

Place the orchid in the new pot, ensuring it sits at the same level as previously (not too deep or too shallow).

- Hold the orchid in place and begin putting the new potting material around the roots, gently pushing it in to eliminate air pockets.

- **Settling the Medium:**

Tap the pot lightly on a hard surface to help settle the medium around the roots.

- Add more medium as needed to fill the container, ensuring the orchid is stable but not unduly compacted.

- **Aftercare:**

Water the orchid sparingly to settle the medium and stimulate root contact.

- Place the repotted orchid in an area with appropriate light and temperature for its species.

- Monitor the orchid closely for the first several weeks, adjusting watering as needed to prevent overwatering or drying out.

Tips for Successful Repotting

- Timing:

Repot orchids during their active growth phase, often in spring or early summer, to minimize stress and enhance recuperation.

- Sanitation:

Always use sterilized utensils and clean pots to prevent the spread of disease.

- Patience:

Allow the orchid time to adjust to its new habitat. It may take a few weeks for fresh root growth and adaptability.

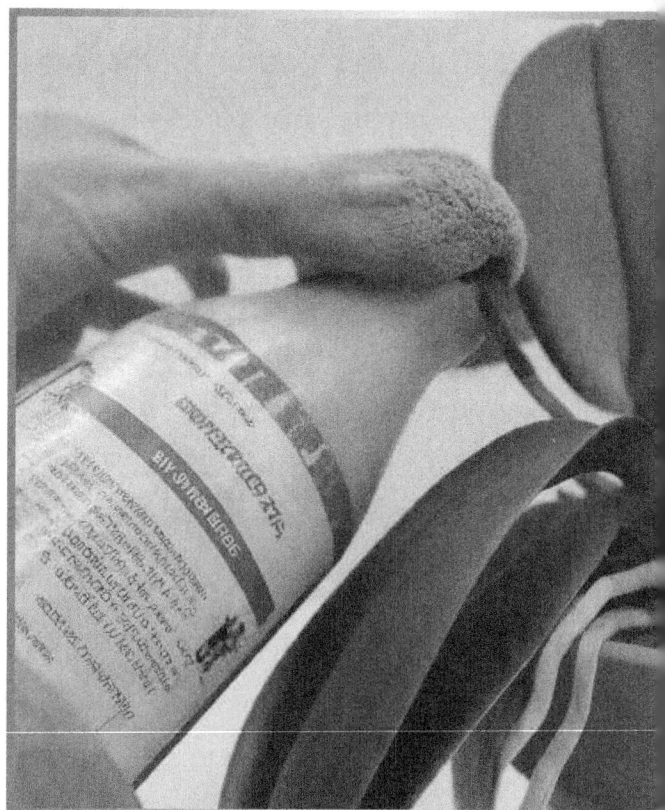

Orchid Care Fundamentals

Chapter 7

Lighting for Orchids (natural and artificial)

Orchids, like all plants, rely on light for photosynthesis, the process by which they transform light energy into chemical energy to power growth and bloom production.

Understanding Light Requirements

Orchids are varied and their light requirements vary substantially among species. Generally, orchids are grouped into three light need groups: low light, medium light, and high light. Knowing the light needs of your unique orchid species is vital for giving the proper conditions.

Low-light orchids, such as Phalaenopsis and Paphiopedilum, flourish in settings that simulate the dappled light of woodland understories. Medium-light orchids, including many Oncidiums and Miltonias, prefer bright, indirect light akin to the borders of woods. High-light orchids, like Cattleyas and Vandas, require bright, direct sunshine equivalent to the highest canopy of tropical forests.

Natural Lighting

Natural light is the preferred source for many orchid gardeners since it closely resembles the conditions orchids experience in their original habitats. However, regulating natural light can be problematic due to fluctuations in intensity and duration throughout the year.

Assessing Natural Light

To properly employ natural light, it's vital to understand the qualities of the light in your growing space. Factors to consider include the direction your windows face, seasonal fluctuations in light intensity, and any obstructions like trees or buildings.

South-facing windows provide the most consistent and powerful light, making them perfect for high-light orchids. East and west-facing windows offer moderate light, perfect for medium-light orchids. North-facing windows often supply little light and are suitable for low-light orchids or as supplemental light sources.

Managing Natural Light

Orchid producers can regulate natural light using many techniques:

- Window Placement: Place orchids near windows that provide the optimum light intensity. Adjust their closeness to the window based on their specific light demands.

- Sheer Curtains: Use sheer curtains to soften bright sunlight, reducing leaf burn while yet providing ample light for photosynthesis.

- Seasonal Adjustments: Move orchids to different spots throughout your home as the seasons change to maintain consistent light exposure. For example, during winter months when light intensity reduces, placing orchids closer to windows can assist in compensating for the lower light.

Signs of Improper Light

Orchids will present unmistakable indicators if they are not receiving the correct quantity of light. Too little light results in dark green, drooping leaves, and a lack of flowering. Conversely, too much light causes yellowing leaves, sunburn patches, and overall plant stress. Monitoring your orchids often and altering their light settings correctly is key for maintaining their health and vibrancy.

Artificial Lighting

Artificial lighting is a useful tool for orchid growers, especially for those who lack sufficient natural light in their houses. With improvements in technology, a range of artificial light sources are available that can successfully augment or replace natural light.

Types of Artificial Lights

Several types of artificial lights are suitable for orchid development, each with its benefits and considerations.

- Fluorescent Lights: Fluorescent lights are a popular choice due to their price and efficiency. They give a broad spectrum of light and emit less heat, making them suitable for orchids. T5 fluorescent bulbs are extremely good for medium and low-light orchids. For optimal results, put the lights 6-12 inches above the plants and utilize reflectors to improve light distribution.

- LED Lights: LED lights have become increasingly popular for their energy economy, extended lifespan, and programmable light spectrums. Full-spectrum LED grow lights resemble natural sunlight and are suited for all species of orchids. LEDs can be positioned closer to the plants without the risk of overheating, often 12-24 inches above the orchids. Some LED systems offer adjustable light spectrums to customize the light conditions to the precise demands of your orchids throughout different growth phases.

High-Intensity Discharge (HID) Lights: HID lights, particularly Metal Halide (MH) and High-Pressure Sodium (HPS) lights, emit powerful light appropriate for high-light orchids. They release tremendous heat and require careful placement and ventilation to avoid overheating.

HID lights are often employed in larger growing setups or greenhouses where their high intensity and coverage area may be fully used.

Setting Up Artificial Lighting

When putting up artificial lighting, consider the following elements to get optimal results:

- **Light Intensity:**

Measure light intensity with a light meter to ensure your orchids receive the optimum quantity of light. Different orchids require varying light levels, commonly measured in foot candles or lux. For example, low-light orchids need roughly 1,000-1,500 foot candles, medium-light orchids need 1,500-3,000 foot candles, and high-light orchids need 3,000-5,000 foot candles.

- **Light Duration:**

Orchids normally need 12-16 hours of light every day. Use timers to automate your lighting routine, guaranteeing regular and enough light exposure. Adjust the period based on the individual demands of your orchids and seasonal fluctuations.

- **Light Spectrum:**

Orchids thrive from a wide spectrum of light, which includes both blue and red wavelengths. Blue light promotes vegetative development, while red light supports flowering. Full-spectrum lights or a combination of different light sources can supply the appropriate wavelengths for healthy orchid growth.

- **Distance and Placement:**

Proper installation of artificial lights is vital to prevent leaf burn and maintain even light dispersion. Follow manufacturer specifications for the recommended distance between the light source and your orchids. Ensure the lights cover the entire plant canopy, using reflectors or additional lights if needed to avoid shadows and uneven growth.

Combining Natural and Artificial Lighting

Combining natural and artificial lighting can provide the best of both worlds, ensuring your orchids receive ample light throughout the year. This strategy is particularly effective during winter months or in dwellings with minimal natural light. Here are several techniques for merging two light sources:

- **Supplemental Lighting:**

Use artificial lights to complement natural light during periods of low intensity or short daylight hours. Position artificial lights to maximize natural light exposure, filling in areas where natural light is insufficient.

- **Seasonal Adjustments:**

Adjust the balance between natural and artificial illumination based on seasonal fluctuations. Increase artificial light usage during winter and reduce it during summer when natural light is more abundant.

- **Light Movements:**

Consider employing light movers to replicate the natural movement of the sun. Light movers can assist spread light more evenly and prevent hotspots, supporting uniform growth.

Monitoring and Adjusting Light Conditions

Consistent monitoring and adjustment of light conditions are crucial for optimal orchid health. Regularly examine your orchids for symptoms of light stress and make appropriate modifications. Investing in a light meter can help you correctly measure light intensity and make informed decisions about light placement and duration.

Chapter 8

Requirements for Humidity and Watering

Because of their many species and intricate care needs, orchids require particular attention to humidity and watering to flourish. **Comprehending these requirements is essential to keeping orchids healthy and producing flowers.**

- ### *Water's Significance to Orchid Health*

Water is essential to orchid development and health. It makes vital functions like temperature regulation, photosynthesis, and nutrition intake easier. However, compared to other houseplants, orchids require a different kind of watering due to their distinctive structure, particularly their roots.

Velum, or spongy tissue, covers the roots of orchids, especially epiphytic orchids. In addition to fast absorbing nutrients and water, this tissue dries quickly, simulating the natural habitat of orchids, which are trees that cling on to moisture from the atmosphere and sporadic rainfall.

- ### *Watering Frequency*

The species of orchid, the potting material, the size of the container, and the surrounding conditions all affect how frequently orchids need to be watered. In general, underwater orchids are preferable to overwater orchids. Watering once a week is a typical recommendation, however, this can change:

1. Phalaenopsis Orchids: These orchids would rather have a little dryness in their roots in between waterings. Usually, one weekly watering is adequate.
2. Dendrobium Orchids: During the growing season, these orchids need to be watered more frequently; however, during the resting phase, they require less watering.

- *Indices of Adequate Watering*

You may learn a lot about your orchid's watering requirements by watching it. Typically, healthy orchids exhibit:

1. Sturdy, green roots that, when dried, have a silvery shine.
2. Thick, plump leaves that don't yellow or wrinkle.
3. Regular cycles of blooming and robust new growth.

On the other hand, moldy or mushy potting medium, yellowing foliage, and root rot can all be signs of overwatering orchids. Underwater orchids can grow more slowly and frequently have withered roots and leaves.

Orchid Watering Techniques

- *Soak Technique*

The soaking method is one efficient way to water orchids. To do this, submerge the orchid pot in a basin of water and let the potting media soak for ten to fifteen minutes. Make sure the pot is completely drained after soaking to avoid water pooling at the bottom.

- *Misting*

Misting orchids can be helpful, especially if they prefer higher humidity levels. Mist the roots and leaves of the orchid sparingly with a fine mist spray. Misting shouldn't take the place of routine watering, though, as it usually doesn't give the roots enough moisture.

- *Ingesting Water from Above*

When watering from above, the potting media is gently covered with water and allowed to drain out the bottom of the pot. By using this technique, water is guaranteed to reach every root system. It's critical to use room temperature water and to refrain from watering the plant's crown, as this can cause crown rot.

- *Using Distilled Water or Rainwater*

Chemicals like fluoride and chlorine that are present in tap water can harm orchids. Rainwater or distilled water are the best options since they closely resemble the natural water that orchids find in their natural habitats. It's best to leave tap water outside for a full day to allow the toxins to break down.

Controlling Humidity in Orchids

- *Humidity's Significance*

Because humidity affects how well orchids absorb water and minerals, it is important for their health. Tropical orchids in particular do well in habitats with greater relative humidity levels, usually between 50% and 70%.

- *Techniques for Raising Humidity*

-Humidity Trays: You can help raise the local humidity by growing orchids on trays that are filled with water and pebbles. Around the plant, a humid microenvironment is produced as the water vapor evaporates.

- Air purifiers: A good option to keep humidity levels steady is to use a humidifier, especially in arid locations or in the winter when the air indoors can get quite dry.

- Organizing Plants: As the orchids evaporate and release moisture into the air, grouping them can result in a more humid atmosphere.

- Stillness: As previously noted, misting can help raise the humidity around the orchids, but for optimal effects, it should be used in concert with other techniques.

- *Keeping an eye on humidity levels*

It is imperative to regularly check the levels of humidity. Hygrometers are practical instruments for determining the humidity level in a growing environment. By keeping the surroundings constant, you can lessen stress on the plants, which promotes healthier growth and blooming.

- ***Handling Reduced Humidity***

In regions where humidity levels are naturally low, further precautions can be required. In addition to keeping doors and windows closed, orchids can be placed in bathrooms or kitchens, which naturally have greater humidity levels, to assist retain humidity.

Temperature and Water Quality

- ***Water Purity***

The health of orchids is greatly impacted by the quality of the water they are kept in. Because tap water contains impurities that can build up in the potting medium and cause poor growth and discolored leaves, orchids prefer clean water sources.

- ***Temperature of Water***

Orchids can be shocked by water that is either too hot or too cold. The best water is lukewarm or room temperature. Hot water can harm the roots and leaves, while cold water can reduce the activity of the roots. Seasonal Variations in Humidity and Watering

- ***The Season of Growth***

Orchids need more frequent watering and greater humidity levels throughout the growing season, which is usually in the spring and summer, to stimulate new growth and flowering. During these months, there is an increase in light levels and warmer temperatures, which causes the potting media to dry out more quickly and the plants to absorb more water.

- ***Inactive Phase***

In contrast, orchids need less regular watering during the dormant season, which typically falls between fall and winter. It is best to let the potting medium dry out more in between waterings, and you can slightly lower the humidity levels. Cooler temperatures and less light cause the plant's metabolic processes to slow down, which lowers the amount of water it needs.

Chapter 9

Managing Nutrients and Fertilization

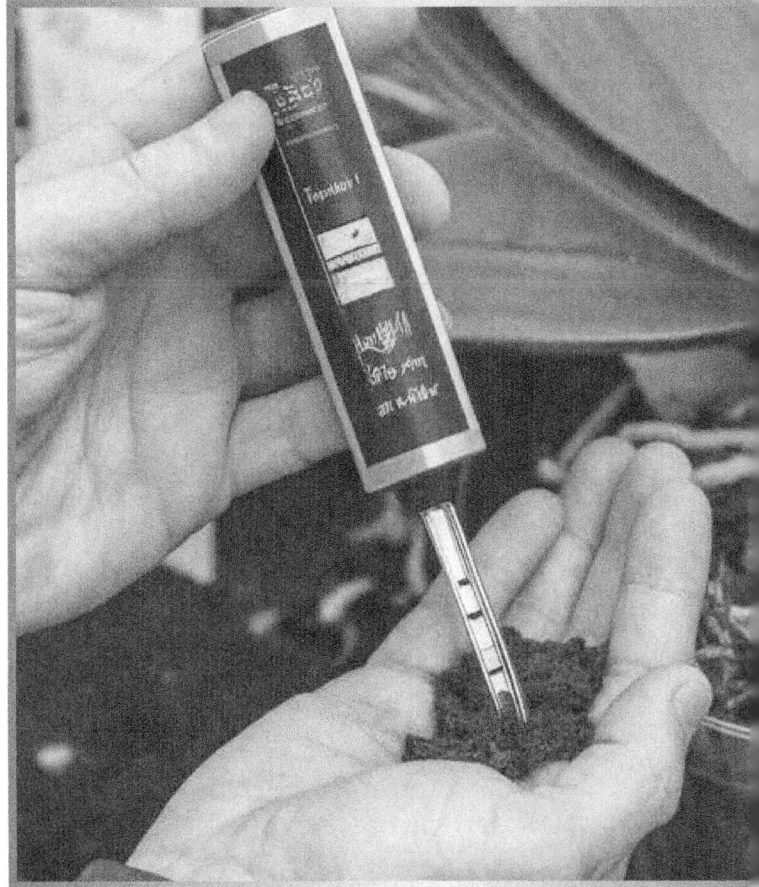

An essential part of orchid care that has a big impact on growth, health, and flowering potential is fertilization. Orchids get the vital components they need for essential part of orchid care that has a big impact on growth, health, and flowering potential is fertilization. Orchids get the vital components they need for

Apart from these essential macronutrients, secondary nutrients including sulfur, calcium, and magnesium are also required by orchids. Trace elements like <u>iron, manganese, zinc, copper, molybdenum, and boron</u> are also necessary for them. Each of these nutrients has a distinct purpose in the physiology of orchids, influencing things like the synthesis of chlorophyll, the activation of enzymes, and cellular activity.

Different Fertilizer Types

Phosphorus, potassium, and nitrogen are all present in equal amounts in balanced fertilizers **(N-P-K),** which are perfect for general-purpose feeding. The ratio of a typical balanced fertilizer could be 10-10-10 or 20-20-20. Conversely, bloom boosters are intended to promote flowering and have a higher phosphorus concentration. They may contain an N-P-K ratio of 10-30-20 or something similar, which makes them very helpful for promoting flower development and longevity throughout the blooming phase.

Fertilizer specifically designed for orchids is made to match their specific requirements; commonly, ratios like *10-10-30 for blooming and 30-10-10* for growth are used. In addition, these fertilizers include extra micronutrients specifically designed for orchids. The nutrients in organic fertilizers are released gradually and come from natural sources.

Fish emulsion, seaweed extract, and compost teas are a few examples of products that enhance the structure and health of the soil, encouraging strong root growth and general plant vitality.

Methods of Application

Fertilizers should be diluted for orchids to avoid nutrient accumulation and root burn. Using a "weakly, weekly" approach—applying a diluted fertilizer solution each week—is a typical technique. Usually, it's enough to use between 25% and 50% of the suggested strength listed on the fertilizer label.

Before fertilization, orchid roots should be well-hydrated so they may receive nutrients without becoming harmed. To prevent oversaturating the potting medium, the diluted fertilizer solution should be sprayed during routine watering sessions.

Foliar feeding is the practice of directly spraying leaves with a diluted fertilizer solution. This promotes rapid nitrogen uptake and is especially helpful in treating nutritional deficits. To minimize leaf burn while using foliar feeding, it is imperative to utilize a fine mist and avoid spraying during the warmest portion of the day.

Another successful technique is root drenching, which involves creating a diluted fertilizer solution and submerging the orchid pot in it for ten to fifteen minutes. After that, complete drainage is essential to avoid waterlogging.

It's also crucial to modify the fertilization schedule by the orchid's growth cycle. Fertilize orchids more frequently throughout the active growing season, which is usually in the spring and summer.

On the other hand, while the orchid's nutritional requirements are lower during the dormant season—typically fall and winter—fertilization should be scaled back or stopped.

Complex Nutrient Methods

Nutrient management strategies must be adjusted seasonally to meet the orchid's varying needs all year round. A greater nitrogen fertilizer promotes leaf and stem growth during the growing season. Changing to a bloom booster with a higher phosphorus content as the orchid gets closer to flowering time will improve flower development.

It is crucial to regularly check the pH levels in the fertilizer and watering solutions since orchids prefer slightly acidic pH values, usually between 5.5 and 6.5, above neutral pH levels. If required, the pH can be lowered with peat moss or sulfur raised with lime.

A lack of certain nutrients can show up in several ways. For example, a nitrogen deficiency can cause older leaves to yellow and stunt growth; a phosphorus deficiency can cause poor root development and delayed flowering; a potassium deficiency can cause weak stems, browning leaf edges, and decreased disease resistance. If shortages are found, modifying the fertilizer schedule or taking supplements made to replace the deficient nutrient can be beneficial.

Micronutrients must also be included for orchid health. Make sure the micronutrient mix in your fertilizer is balanced, or add more as needed. Orchids tend to absorb chelated micronutrient formulations more easily.

The Best Ways to Fertilize Orchids

It is essential to use high-quality fertilizers made especially for orchids, as general-purpose plant fertilizers might not be able to satisfy the needs of orchids. The key to giving orchids the nutrients they require over time is consistency, which can only be achieved by creating and following a regular fertilization regimen.

It's important to regularly check your orchids for indicators of toxicity or nutrient stress. Maintaining optimal health can be achieved by modifying the fertilization schedule according to the plant's response and growth stage. Maintaining a healthy root environment is made possible by routinely rinsing the potting media with plain water to minimize the development of salts and minerals from fertilizers.

It's critical to modify your fertilization techniques to your orchids' seasonal development cycle, boosting nutrient availability during active growth and decreasing it during dormancy. You can adjust your fertilizing strategy to meet the unique requirements of each orchid species you cultivate by realizing that different orchid species have varied nutrient requirements.

Useful Advice for Efficient Nutrition Management

- It is important to measure fertilizer dilution accurately to avoid giving your orchids too much or too little. Fertilizers stay effective if they are stored properly in a dry, cool environment. A comprehensive distribution of nutrients is ensured by combining several fertilizing techniques, such as root drenching and foliar feeding.

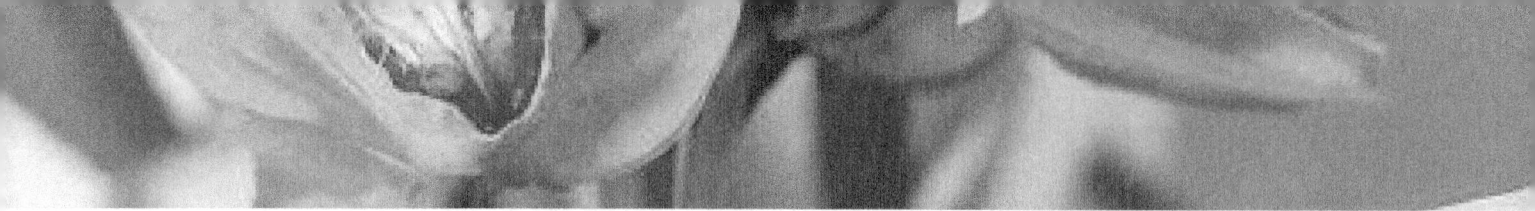

Chapter 10
Pruning and Grooming Orchids

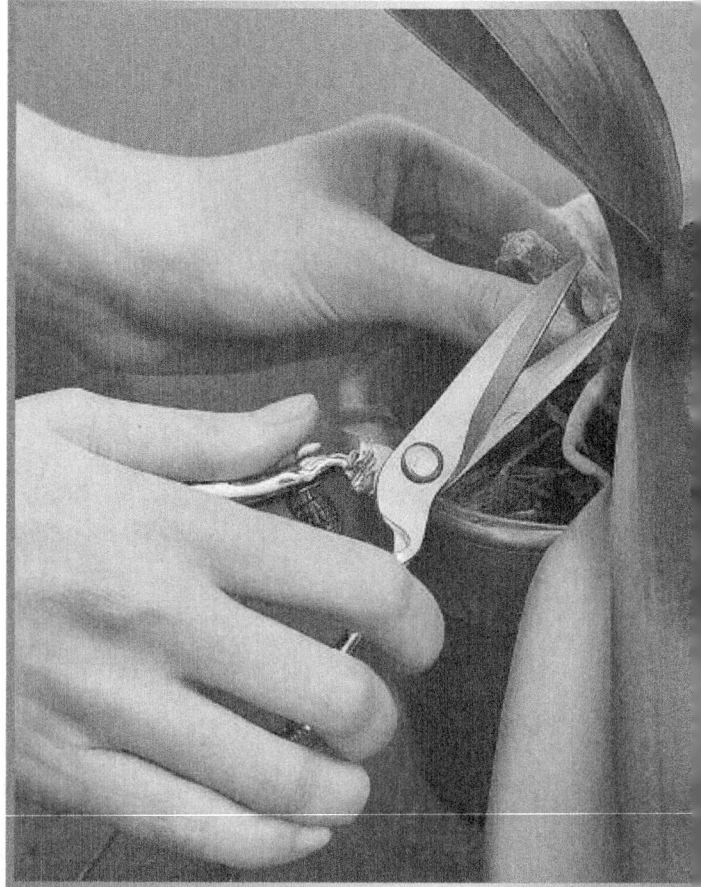

Pruning and grooming a plant properly can help reduce the danger of pests and illnesses by removing dead, damaged, or diseased areas, encouraging new growth, and improving airflow around the plant.

The Value of Grooming and Pruning

Maintaining the health and beauty of orchids requires regular pruning and maintenance. These care procedures guarantee that the plant keeps its attractive appearance, promotes vigorous blooming, and stops the spread of illness. Frequent pruning helps the plant focus its energy on new growth by getting rid of damaged or dead leaves as well as discarded blossoms. On the other side, grooming keeps the plant dust-free and clean, which improves its capacity for efficient photosynthetic processes.

Understanding The Structure of Orchids

Monopodial and sympodial orchids are the two basic kinds into which orchids fall.

- Orchids with monopods:

These orchids have linearly organized leaves and grow vertically from a single stem. Monopodial orchids include Phalaenopsis and Vanda species. In between the leaves on the stem, they develop flower spikes.

- Orchids in Sympodial:

These orchids produce new growth from a rhizome and grow horizontally. Cattleya, Dendrobium, and Oncidium orchids are a few examples. Sympodial orchids have enlarged stems called pseudobulbs that serve as nutritional and water storage units. From the base of older pseudobulbs, new growth appears.

It is essential to comprehend these development patterns to use the proper grooming and trimming strategies.

Techniques for Pruning

- Removing Flower Spike Spills:

Orchids may have discolored, withered flower spikes after they have finished blooming. Cut the flower spike of monopodial orchids, such as Phalaenopsis, approximately 0.5 inches above the closest node or joint on the spike. As a result, the plant is encouraged to grow new flower spikes from the node. After blooming is finished, clip the flower spike of sympodial orchids, such as Cattleya and Dendrobium, back to the base of the pseudobulb. This aids in refocusing the plant's energy on upcoming flowers and new developments.

- Cutting Off Damaged or Dead Roots:

Dead orchid roots are soft, brown, or black, but healthy roots are solid and white or green. Examine the roots of the orchid after carefully removing it from its pot. Remove any damaged or dead roots with sterile scissors or pruning shears. By doing this, you can stop root rot from spreading and promote the development of new, healthy roots.

- Removing Sick or Damaged Leaves:

Diseases and injuries can occasionally affect orchid leaves. Using sterile scissors, trim any yellowed, brown, or blackened leaves, making sure to cut as near to the base as possible to avoid damaging the surrounding healthy tissue. Eliminating these leaves makes the plant aesthetically pleasing and stops the spread of illness.

- Parting Entire Orchids:

In their pots, symbols orchids can get congested as they generate more pseudobulbs. These orchids are rejuvenated and given more room to flourish when they are divided.

To divide, take the orchid out of its pot and carefully split the rhizome into sections, making sure that each has a good root system and three pseudobulbs at least. Each division should be replanted with new potting material in an appropriate pot.

Grooming Methodologies

- Orchid Leaf Cleaning:

On orchid leaves, dust and debris can build up, impeding photosynthesis and increasing the plant's vulnerability to pests. Using a gentle, moist cloth, regularly wipe the leaves clean. Use a solution of one part milk to two parts water for a more thorough cleaning that leaves the leaves with a natural gloss and helps eliminate residue.

- Investigating Bloom Spikes:

Orchids may require support as their flower spikes enlarge to keep them from bending or breaking. To gently support the flower spikes, use clips and stakes. Stake the spike in the potting medium close to its base, then use clips or soft ties to hold it in place. Take care not to harm the spike itself or the roots.

- Treating Roots Aerial:

Many orchid species, particularly epiphytic orchids like Phalaenopsis, have aerial roots. These roots assist the plant in absorbing moisture from the atmosphere as they extend above the potting media. Even though aerial roots are a necessary component of an orchid's growth, they can occasionally become uncontrollably large or unattractive. If necessary, use sterile scissors to clip back lengthy aerial roots; do not remove them completely, as they are essential to the life of the plant.

Pruning and Grooming Best Practices

- Using sanitized Tools:

To stop the spread of illness, always use pruning shears or scissors that have been sanitized. Before and after usage, sterilize instruments with rubbing alcohol or a weak solution of bleach.

- Taking Strict Measures:

To encourage rapid healing and lower the risk of infection, make sure cuts are accurate and clean. Plants with jagged cuts may be more susceptible to disease.

Sowing in the Dormant Seasons: When orchids are dormant, usually after blooming, they should be pruned and groomed. The plant may recuperate and concentrate its energy on new growth and blossoming during this time.

- Observation and Patience:

Orchid development might be sluggish, so exercise patience and diligence. Keep a regular eye on the condition and appearance of your orchids, and make any necessary adjustments to your pruning and grooming techniques.

Seasonal Pruning and Grooming

- *Summer and Spring:*

More regular grooming is beneficial for orchids throughout their active growing season. Take off any damaged or dead growth, then use stakes to hold the newly planted flower spikes. It's crucial to regularly wipe the leaves and keep an eye out for pests during this time of rapid development.

- *Winter and Fall:*

Cut back on the amount of pruning and grooming when orchids go into dormancy. Make sure to get rid of any dead foliage and any leftover spent flower spikes.

Advanced Orchid Care

Chapter 11
Temperature Control and Seasonal Variations

Orchids come from different environments with distinct temperatures and seasonal patterns, and reproducing these variables in your growing environment is vital to keeping healthy plants and ensuring abundant blooming.

Understanding Orchid Temperature Preferences

Orchids can be roughly divided based on their temperature preferences into three categories: cool-growing, intermediate-growing, and warm-growing. Each category has unique conditions that must be followed to enable optimal growth and flowering.

- **Cool-growing Orchids:**

These orchids flourish in lower temperatures. They normally like daytime temperatures between 55-75°F (13-24°C) and nocturnal temperatures between 50-55°F (10-13°C). Examples include Cymbidium and Masdevallia. These orchids frequently come from high-altitude places where temperatures are naturally lower.

- **Intermediate-growing Orchids:**

These orchids prefer moderate conditions, with daily temperatures between 65-80°F (18-27°C) and nocturnal temperatures between 55-65°F (13-18°C). Examples include Cattleya and Oncidium. These orchids are often found in mid-elevation areas with modest temperature variations.

- **Warm-growing Orchids:**

These orchids flourish in warmer temperatures, preferring daytime temperatures between 75-85°F (24-29°C) and nocturnal temperatures between 65-70°F (18-21°C). Examples include Phalaenopsis and Vanda. These orchids originate from lowland tropical locations where temperatures remain continuously high.

Strategies for Effective Temperature Control

Maintaining the optimum temperature range for your orchids involves numerous ways to produce a stable environment that replicates their native habitats.

- **Thermometers and Hygrometers:**

Regularly monitoring temperature and humidity levels is vital. Place thermometers and hygrometers in different places in your growing area to acquire a full understanding of the environmental conditions.

- **Heating Systems:**

During colder months, especially for chilly and intermediate-growing orchids, it may be necessary to employ additional heating. Space heaters, heating mats, and heat lamps can give the essential warmth. Ensure that these heating devices are equally distributed and do not produce hot patches that could damage the orchids.

- **Cooling Systems:**

In warmer climates or during the summer, cooling systems may be needed to keep temperatures within the optimal range. Fans, air conditioners, and evaporative coolers can assist reduce the temperature. Ensure good air circulation to prevent stagnant air, which can lead to fungal illnesses.

- **Ventilation:**

Proper ventilation is vital for maintaining temperature regulation. Use oscillating fans to guarantee even air distribution around the orchids. Good airflow helps to manage temperature and humidity, minimizing the risk of infections.

- **Insulation:**

In greenhouses or indoor growth environments, insulation can help maintain a constant temperature. During winter, insulation helps retain heat, while in summer, it can keep excessive heat out.

Reflective materials and shade cloths can also be used to adjust light and temperature levels.

- **Natural Temperature Variation:**

Allow for natural temperature swings between day and night. Most orchids thrive from a decrease of roughly 10-15°F (5-8°C) at night. This diurnal variation is critical for triggering flowering in many orchid species.

Adapting to Seasonal Changes

Orchids suffer seasonal variations in their natural environments, and adjusting to these changes in your cultivation procedures is vital for their health and blooming cycles. Each season provides various requirements for temperature management and care.

Spring:

- development Phase: Many orchids undergo a period of active development in spring. Increase watering and fertilizing to stimulate new growth. Ensure they receive ample light, as longer daytime hours stimulate rapid growth.

- Temperature Management: Maintain suitable temperatures, ensuring that daytime temperatures do not exceed the ideal range for your orchid species. Use shade cloths and fans to prevent overheating.

Summer:

- Peak Growing Season: Orchids continue their active development during summer. Regularly check for symptoms of overheating, such as wilting or leaf burn. Provide ample shade and increase watering frequency to keep up with warmer temperatures and increased transpiration.

- Cooling Measures: Use fans and air conditioners to keep temperatures within the optimal range. Good air circulation is vital to prevent heat accumulation and lower the danger of fungal infections.

Fall:

- Transition to Dormancy: Some orchids begin to slow down their growth as they prepare for dormancy. Gradually minimize watering and fertilizing to reflect the plant's lower metabolic activity.

- Temperature Adjustment: Allow temperatures to drop somewhat to replicate the cooler conditions of the orchid's natural habitat. This helps trigger blooming in species like Cymbidium and Dendrobium which require a chilly period to develop flower buds.

Winter:

- Dormant Phase: During winter, many orchids enter a dormant phase with low growth. Reduce watering to prevent root rot, but ensure the roots do not dry out completely. Non-dormant orchids may still require regular watering, albeit less frequently than during the growing season.

- Maintaining Warmth: Use heaters and insulation to keep orchids warm, especially in cooler locations. Ensure that nighttime temperatures do not drop too low, as this can cause stress and damage to the plants.

Chapter 12
Pest and Disease Management

BY Knowing these problems and implementing integrated pest management measures, you may maintain a thriving orchid collection.

Identifying Common Orchid Pests

Orchids are subject to several pests, each with particular traits and damage patterns.

- **Aphids**

Aphids are little, soft-bodied insects that can be green, black, or brown. They tend to congregate on new growth and flower buds, feasting on plant sap. Symptoms of aphid infestation include the presence of sticky honeydew on leaves, deformed new growth, and the formation of sooty mold. To handle aphids, you can treat the infected plants with insecticidal soap or neem oil. Introducing natural predators like ladybugs can also help manage aphid populations.

- **Mealybugs**

Mealybugs are little, white, cottony insects that attach themselves to leaves, stems, and roots. Infestations result in reduced development, yellowing leaves, and sticky residue. Mealybugs can be removed manually with a cotton swab dipped in alcohol. For heavier infestations, use horticultural oil or insecticidal soap in the afflicted regions.

- **Spider Mites**

Spider mites are tiny red or brown arachnids that typically seem like moving dots. They flourish in dry circumstances and are frequently found on the undersides of leaves. Signs of spider mite damage include thin webbing, stippled or discolored leaves, and leaf drop. To manage spider mites, boost humidity around your plants, wash leaves with water, and apply miticides or insecticidal soap.

- **Scale Insects**

Scale insects are hard or soft shell-covered bugs that cling to stems and leaves, draining plant sap. This results in yellowing leaves and sticky residue, which might attract sooty mold. Scale can be controlled by manually removing them with a cotton swab dipped in alcohol. For serious infestations, apply horticultural oil or systemic insecticides.

- **Thrips**

Thrips are tiny, slender insects that are generally black or yellow. They eat on flowers and leaves, causing silver streaks or scars and malformed buds. To manage thrips, use sticky traps to check their presence, boost humidity, and apply insecticidal soap or spinosad as needed.

- **Slugs and Snails**

Slugs and snails are soft-bodied mollusks that nibble on leaves and flowers, leaving ragged holes and slime trails. To control these pests, handpick them at night when they are active, use copper tape barriers around pots, and apply iron phosphate-based baits.

Identifying Common Orchid Diseases

Orchids are also subject to various illnesses, primarily caused by fungi, bacteria, and viruses.

- **Fungal Infections**

Fungal diseases can cause substantial damage to orchids if not addressed promptly. Common fungal illnesses include black rot and leaf spot.

- **Black Rot**

Black rot, caused by Pythium and Phytophthora fungus, displays as black, mushy roots or pseudobulbs, leading to fast plant loss.

To control black rot, remove and discard affected sections, promote air circulation around the plants, minimize overwatering, and apply appropriate fungicides.

- **Leaf Spot**

Leaf spot diseases, caused by fungi such as Cercospora and Botrytis, show as brown or black dots on leaves, typically surrounded by yellow halos. Managing leaf spots entails removing infected leaves, increasing air circulation, and spraying fungicides to prevent further spread.

- **Bacterial Infections**

Bacterial infections can quickly damage orchid plants. Two frequent bacterial illnesses include bacterial soft spot and bacterial brown spot.

- **Microbially Soft Spot**

Bacterial soft spot, which is caused by Erwinia bacteria, appears as smooth, wet lesions on leaves or pseudobulbs and is frequently accompanied by an unpleasant smell. Applying bactericides, avoiding overhead watering, using sterile instruments, and removing affected tissue right away are the best ways to manage bacterial soft spots.

- **Infectious Brown Patch**

Brown, water-soaked sores on leaves are the hallmark of bacterial brown spots, which are brought on by Acidovorax. Applying copper-based bactericides, increasing air circulation, and removing contaminated tissue are all necessary for managing this illness.

- **Viral Diseases**

Mosaic viruses, like Cymbidium Mosaic Virus (CyMV) and Orchid Fleck Virus (OFV), create twisted flowers and leaves that are mottled, streaked, or flecked. Sadly, viral infections have no known treatment. Using sterilized instruments and getting rid of contaminated plants will stop the spread and safeguard the remainder of your collection.

Best Practices and Preventive Actions

It is significantly more beneficial to prevent diseases and pests than to treat them. You can lessen your chance of diseases and infestations by adhering to these best practices.

- **Consistent Observation**

Check your orchids once a week for any indications of illness or pests. Focus especially on the undersides of leaves, buds, and new growth. Early detection makes it possible to act quickly and stop minor issues from growing into larger ones.

- **Isolate Fresh Plants**

Before adding new plants to your collection, always isolate them for a minimum of two weeks. Watch them carefully for any indications of illness or pests throughout this quarantine time. This procedure aids in keeping your established plants from picking up new issues.

- **Adequate Hygiene**

Keep the growth environment tidy. When cutting or repotting orchids, use sterile instruments, and make sure to routinely clean and sanitize growth spaces and equipment. Diseases and pests are less likely to spread when there is proper sanitation.

- **Environmental Management**

Make sure there is enough airflow around your plants to avoid bacterial and fungal diseases. Plants should not be overcrowded as this might lead to an infestation of pests and the spread of disease.

- **Adequate Watering Techniques**

If you water your orchids early in the day, the leaves will have time to dry before dusk. Keep the potting medium dry; too much moisture might cause root rot. Adhering to appropriate irrigation techniques promotes disease prevention and plant health.

- **Utilizing Natural Predators**

To organically manage pest populations, introduce beneficial insects like ladybugs, predatory mites, and lacewings. Predators like these can aid in controlling insect populations without the use of chemical treatments.

- **Chemical Restraints**

Use chemical controls, such as systemic insecticides, horticultural oils, and insecticidal soaps, when needed. To stop pests from becoming resistant, carefully read the label directions and switch up the pesticides you use.

- **Incorporated Termite Care (ITC)**

To efficiently manage pests and illnesses, integrated pest management (IPM) is a comprehensive technique that incorporates chemical, biological, and cultural strategies.

- **Cultural Restraints**

Orchids experience less stress when growing circumstances are kept healthy, which makes them less vulnerable to illnesses and pests. To encourage healthy growth, make sure to provide enough light, air movement, and watering.

- **Biocontrol Mechanisms**

To control pest populations, use helpful microbes and natural predators. For instance, it may be useful to introduce ladybugs to manage aphids or predatory mites to control spider mites.

- **Mechanisms of Control**

To stop infestations and diseases from spreading, manually remove pests and unhealthy plant portions. This technique works especially well for visible pests such as mealybugs, snails, and slugs.

- **Chemical Restraints**

Use fungicides and pesticides sparingly, emphasizing targeted rather than broad-spectrum treatments. For a well-rounded approach, use chemical controls in addition to other techniques and as a last resort.

- **Urgent Interventions**

To reduce damage in the event of an infestation of a pest or illness, quick action is necessary.

- **Seclusion**

To stop the disease from spreading to healthy plants, separate afflicted plants very away. This is a crucial step in keeping the issue under control and safeguarding the remainder of your collection.

- Intervention

By the type of pest or disease found, use the proper therapies. If more treatments are required, continue as before and keep a watchful eye out for any indications of progress or new problems.

- **Removal**

Plants that have been severely infected or infested may need to be disposed of. Remove diseased plants from your growing space safely to avoid contaminating it.

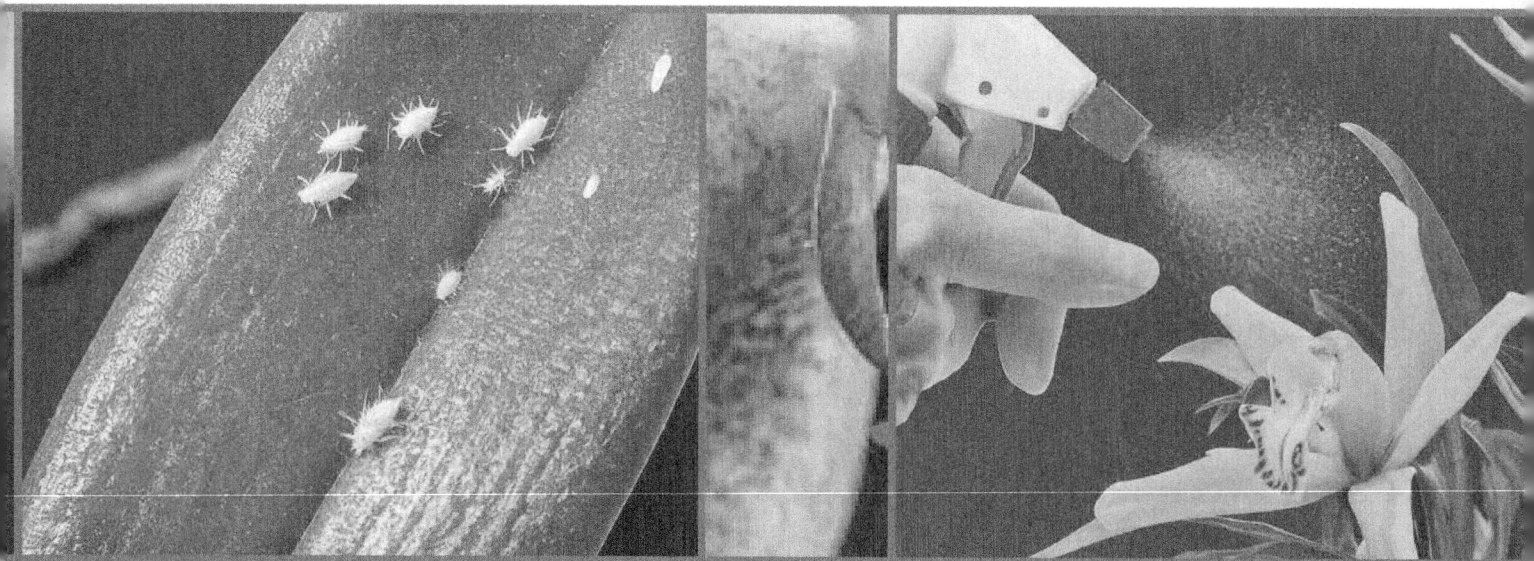

Chapter 13

Growing and Cross-breeding Orchids

With the use of cutting-edge techniques like hybridization and propagation, orchid aficionados can grow their collections and produce new types.

Strategies for Propagation

Growing new plants from old ones is called propagation. There are various ways to reproduce orchids, such as division, keikis, back bulbs, and seed propagation. Every approach has particular stages and prerequisites.

Division

One of the most popular ways to propagate sympodial orchids, like Cattleya and Dendrobium, is by division.

- **Actions:**
1. Select the Appropriate Time: After flowering, when repotting is taking place, is the ideal moment to divide orchids.
2. Set Up the Plant: Take out the orchid from its container and give the old potting material a little shake.
3. Identify Natural Divisions: Where new growth has appeared in the rhizome, look for natural divisions.
4. Cut the Rhizome: Make sure each division has at least three to four pseudobulbs by cutting the rhizome in between them with a sterile knife or pair of scissors.
5. Pot the Divisions: Ensure that the pseudobulbs are above the medium level by placing each division in a different pot filled with fresh potting medium.
6. Treating the Divisions: After giving the just potted divisions a little water until new growth shows, return to giving them frequent attention.

Backbulbs

The older, leafless pseudobulbs known as back bulbs are useful for multiplying sympodial orchids.

- **Actions:**

1. Select Backbulbs: From the orchid, select firm, healthy backbulbs.
2. Set Up the Backbulbs: Using a sterile instrument, cut the backbulbs from the main plant.
3. Contain the Backbulbs: Lay the backbulbs in a container horizontally on a layer of bark mixture or sphagnum moss.
4. Maintain Humidity: To promote growth, cover the pot with a plastic bag or put it in a humid area.
5. Watch and Take Care of When new roots and shoots appear, move the growth to a pot of its own and fill it with the proper potting soil.

Keikis

Keikis are tiny plantlets that typically appear on the nodes of Phalaenopsis and Dendrobium orchid stems.

- **Steps:**

1. Identify Keikis: On the orchid stem, look for little plantlets with roots and leaves sprouting on them.
2. Allow Growth: Permit the keiki to grow until it has many roots that are about 2-3 inches long and at least 2-3 leaves.
3. Remove the Keiki: Cut the keiki from the mother plant, leaving some of the stem attached, using sterile scissors.
4. Pot the Keiki: Make sure the roots of the keiki are covered by adding potting medium to a small pot.
5. Treat the Keiki with care: To promote growth, keep the humidity high and give the right amount of light and water.

Seed Distribution

Because orchids produce small, dust-like seeds that lack nutrient stores, seed propagation is a more sophisticated procedure that requires patience and sterile conditions.

- **Procedure:**
  1. Selection of Seeds: Gather seeds from an established orchid seed pod.
  2. Sterilize Seeds: Use hydrogen peroxide or a weak bleach solution to sterilize the seeds.
  3. Prepare a Sterile Medium: Fill flasks or jars with a nutrient-rich, sterile agar medium.
  4. Sow the Seeds: Place the seeds onto the agar medium in a sterile setting.
  5. Incubate: Close the jars or flasks and set them in a room that is warm and well-lit.
  6. Treatment of Seedlings: The seeds will germinate over a few months, growing into protocorms and then tiny seedlings.
  7. Transplant Seedlings: Move the seedlings to a sterile potting medium for additional growth after they have a few leaves and roots.

Creating Hybrid Orchids

To produce a new type of orchid, hybridization entails cross-pollinating two distinct orchid species or hybrids. This method calls for patience, careful attention to detail, and an understanding of orchid genetics.

- **Choosing Mother Plants**

Selecting appropriate parent plants is essential for a successful hybridization process.

Take into account the following elements:

- Health and Vigor: Choose robustly growing, disease- and pest-free plants that exhibit good health.
- Desirable features: Select plants whose flower color, shape, scent, or size are among the features you wish to blend.

The Pollination Method

1. Identify Flower Parts: Recognize the components of orchid blooms, particularly the stigma (the female part), the anther (the male part), and the column (which houses the reproductive organs).
2. Collect Pollen: Carefully extract the pollinia, or pollen sacs, from the anther of the first parent plant using a sterile toothpick or tweezers.
3. Pollinate: Carefully place the pollinia on the second parent plant's stigma, making sure it adheres to the adhesive surface.
4. Label the Cross: Write the names of both parent plants and the pollination date on the blossom that was pollinated.
5. Keep an eye on the seed pod: The pollinated flower will wither over several weeks to months, and a seed pod will form. Depending on the type of orchid, it may take many months for the pod to mature.

Gathering & Planting Seeds

- Harvest Seeds:

Carefully remove the seed pod to avoid losing any of its seeds as it reaches maturity and starts to split.

- Sterilize and Sow:

Adhere to the previously described seed propagation procedures, making sure that the environment is sterile for effective germination.

- Cultivate Seedlings:

Before transferring seedlings to pots, observe their development under sterile circumstances.

Assessing Upcoming Hybrids

1. Grow and Bloom:
2. As the hybrid seedlings reach maturity, which may need a few years, watch for their first blossoms.
3. Assess Traits:
4. Check for desired characteristics in the new hybrid, like flower color, shape, scent, and general health of the plant.
5. Select and Propagate:
6. Pick the hybrids that are performing the best so they can be entered into orchid shows and registries or continue to propagate them.

Documentation and Record-Keeping

1. Keeping thorough records of your hybridization and propagation activities is crucial to monitoring your progress.
2. Label Plants and Crosses:
3. Put parent names and dates on all propagated and hybridized plants using legible, long-lasting labels.
4. Keep a Log:
5. Document all propagation and hybridizing efforts in writing or digitally, including dates, techniques, and results.

Chapter 14
Nutrient Strategies and Advanced Fertilization

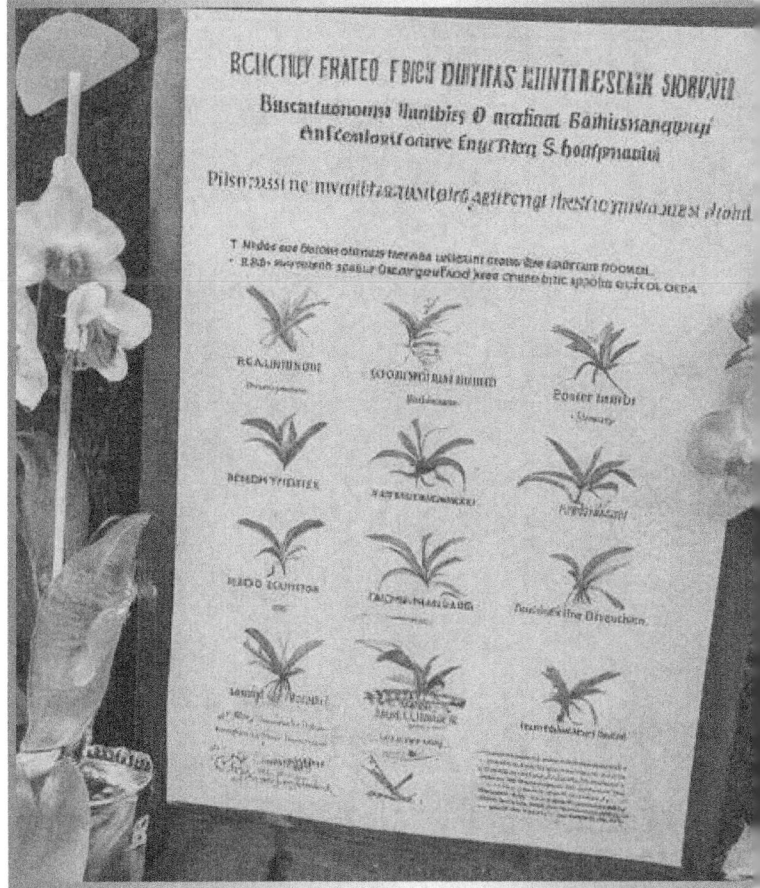

The dietary requirements of orchids are distinct from those of many other houseplants. For them to support different physiological processes, a balanced combination of macronutrients and micronutrients is needed.

Macronutrients

Nitrogen (N):

- Crucial to the growth of leaves and stems.
- Encourages rich, verdant vegetation.

Phosphorus (P):

- Essential for the growth of roots and the generation of flowers.
- Promotes the storage and transfer of energy.

K (potassium):

- Promotes general plant health and disease resistance.
- Enhances enzyme activation and water absorption.

Micronutrients

Calcium (Ca):

- Promotes root and shoot growth and fortifies cell walls.

Magnesium (Mg):

- An essential element for photosynthesis, magnesium is the core of chlorophyll.

Iron (Fe):

- Essential to the synthesis of chlorophyll and the general health of plants.

Other Micronutrients:

- Each of these elements has a distinct function in the health of plants, including boron (B), manganese (Mn), zinc (Zn), copper (Cu), molybdenum (Mo), and chlorine (Cl).

Fertilizer Types

Advanced orchid care requires an understanding of various fertilizer kinds and how to utilize them appropriately.

- Balanced Fertilizers:

Equal amounts of N, P, and K are found in balanced fertilizers (e.g., 20-20-20). They are appropriate for general upkeep when growth is vigorous.

- High-Nitrogen Fertilizers:

Fertilizers with a higher nitrogen content, such as 30-10-10, are perfect for the growing season since they encourage vegetative development.

- Bloom Boosters:

Fertilizers with high phosphorus content, like 10-30-20, are beneficial for flower production and work best when applied in the blooming stage.

- Slow-Release Fertilizers:

By releasing nutrients gradually over time, these granular fertilizers minimize the chance of overfertilization and offer a consistent supply of nutrients.

Methods of Application:

When fertilizers are applied correctly, orchids can get the nutrients plants require without running the risk of nutrient burn or shortage.

Frequency and Dilution:

- Dilution: Because orchids are sensitive to high nutrient concentrations, liquid fertilizers should always be diluted to half or quarter strength.
- Frequency: During the active growing season, fertilize every 1-2 weeks; during dormancy, fertilize less frequently.

Fertilizer Types

Advanced orchid care requires an understanding of various fertilizer kinds and how to utilize them appropriately.

- Balanced Fertilizers:

Equal amounts of N, P, and K are found in balanced fertilizers (e.g., 20-20-20). They are appropriate for general upkeep when growth is vigorous.

- High-Nitrogen Fertilizers:

Fertilizers with a higher nitrogen content, such as 30-10-10, are perfect for the growing season since they encourage vegetative development.

- Bloom Boosters:

Fertilizers with high phosphorus content, like 10-30-20, are beneficial for flower production and work best when applied in the blooming stage.

- Slow-Release Fertilizers:

By releasing nutrients gradually over time, these granular fertilizers minimize the chance of overfertilization and offer a consistent supply of nutrients.

Methods of Application:

When fertilizers are applied correctly, orchids can get the nutrients plants require without running the risk of nutrient burn or shortage.

Frequency and Dilution:

- Dilution: Because orchids are sensitive to high nutrient concentrations, liquid fertilizers should always be diluted to half or quarter strength.
- Frequency: During the active growing season, fertilize every 1-2 weeks; during dormancy, fertilize less frequently.

Foliar Feeding:

Applying a diluted fertilizer solution straight to the leaves is known as foliar feeding. This technique is especially helpful when the roots are not absorbing nutrients as well as they should because it might give them a fast boost.

Root Drenching:

Applying a diluted fertilizer solution to the potting medium is known as "root drenching." The most popular way of fertilizing orchids guarantees that the roots have access to nutrients.

Customized Dietary Plans

To maximize orchid health, different growth stages and environmental factors call for different nutrient methods.

Stage of Seedlings:

For seedlings to sustain their early growth, the right ratio of nutrients must be provided.

- Apply a quarter-strength dilution of a balanced fertilizer.
- To prevent overfeeding, use fertilizer every two to three weeks.
- Make sure there is enough light and high humidity to promote growth.

Stage of Vegetative Growth:

Orchids concentrate on growing leaves and roots during the vegetative growth stage.

- Apply a half-strength fertilizer with a high nitrogen content.
- Fertilize to support strong growth every one to two weeks.
- Supply enough light and keep humidity levels at ideal levels.

Blooming Phase:

For the development of their blooms, flowering orchids require more phosphorus.

- Use a fertilizer diluted to half strength as a bloom booster.
- Fertilize during the blooming time every two weeks.
- Maintain steady temperatures and regular watering to promote flowers.

Lazy Phase:

After blooming, a lot of orchids go into hibernation.

- Either stop fertilizing completely or cut back to once a month.
- If necessary, use a quarter-strength balanced fertilizer.
- Water the plant less often and give it time to relax.

Customized Nutritional Approaches

Specific nutrition techniques may be needed for certain orchid species and growing environments.

Epiphytic Orchids:

Because of their particular growing conditions, epiphytic orchids like Phalaenopsis and Cattleya have particular nutrient requirements.

- During active growth, use a balanced or high-nitrogen fertilizer.
- To replicate the natural absorption of nutrients, use foliar feeding in addition to root drenching.
- Make sure there is adequate airflow and steer clear of soggy potting material.

Terrestrial Orchids:

Cymbidium and other terrestrial orchids are soil-dwelling plants with distinct nutrient needs.

- Make use of a balanced fertilizer that contains a little bit more phosphorus.
- Add organic matter to the soil to increase the availability of nutrients.

- For ideal nutrient uptake, keep an eye on the pH of the soil and make necessary adjustments.

Hydroponic Orchids:

Hydroponically growing orchids necessitates careful nutrient solution control.

- Make use of an orchid-specific hydroponic fertilizer.
- Regularly check and modify the electrical conductivity (EC) and pH of the nutrition solution.
- To avoid nutrient imbalances, swap out the nutrient solution every two to four weeks.

Advanced Fertilization Techniques

More experienced orchid gardeners may use other methods to improve orchid growth even more.

Micronutrient Supplements:

Micronutrients are present in conventional fertilizers, but deficits can be filled in with specialized micronutrient supplements.

- For improved absorption, use chelated versions of calcium, magnesium, and iron.
- Include supplements in your regular fertilization schedule or use them as foliar sprays.

Organic Fertilizers:

Seaweed extract and fish emulsion are examples of organic fertilizers that offer a natural supply of nutrients.

- To offer a wide range of nutrients, combine organic and synthetic fertilizers.
- Apply as a foliar spray or root drench, adhering to the manufacturer's recommendations.

<u>Mycorrhizal Inoculants:</u>

By forming advantageous associations with orchid roots, mycorrhizal fungi improve nutrient intake.

- When repotting orchids, inoculate them with mycorrhizal fungus.
- Use items designed especially for orchids to make sure they work well together.
- Sustain the right amount of moisture to encourage the growth of mycorrhizae.

<u>Monitoring and Adjusting Nutrient Strategies:</u>

To make sure your orchids are getting the nutrients they need, regular observation and modification are essential.

<u>Visual Inspection:</u>

Check your orchids frequently for symptoms of excess or deficiency in nutrients, such as yellowing leaves, slowed growth, or leaf burn.

<u>Soil and Water Testing:</u>

Check the pH and nutrient content of your potting medium and water supply regularly.

- Modify pH levels to keep them between 5.5 and 6.5 for best nutritional absorption.
- Adjust your fertilization schedule in response to test findings to correct any imbalances.

<u>Record Keeping:</u>

Maintain thorough records of your fertilization procedures, including the kinds and quantities of fertilizers applied, the techniques utilized, and the reactions of the plants you see. Over time, you can use this data to improve your nutrient plans.

Specific Orchid Care

Chapter 15

Phalaenopsis and Moth Orchids

Origins and Characteristics

Native to Southeast Asia's tropical regions, phalaenopsis orchids love the warm, muggy weather there. Their common name comes from their graceful, arching flower sprays, which are akin to moths' fragile wings.

The thick, leathery leaves of these orchids are usually grouped in a rosette at the base of the plant. The long, thin stalks carrying the flowers display a range of hues, such as white, pink, purple, and yellow, frequently adorned with elaborate designs and patterns. Individual Phalaenopsis orchid blossoms can last anywhere from a few weeks to many months, and they bloom sporadically throughout the year.

Cultivation Techniques

Paying close attention to the unique environmental and cultural requirements of Phalaenopsis orchids is essential for their successful cultivation.

- Light Requirements

Bright, indirect light is preferred by Phalaenopsis orchids. To give them enough light without subjecting them to direct sunlight, which can result in leaf burn, place them next to windows facing east or west.

- Humidity and Temperature

Maintain temperatures of 70–85°F (21–29°C) during the day and 60–65°F (15–18°C) at night. Phalaenopsis orchids prefer high humidity levels of between 50 and 70 percent.

- Repeating and Potting Medium

A well-draining potting medium, like bark mix or sphagnum moss, is necessary to guarantee sufficient moisture retention and aeration. Every one to two years or when the potting medium degrades, repot Phalaenopsis orchids.

Watering

Usually, every 7 to 10 days, when the potting media is dry to the touch, thoroughly water Phalaenopsis orchids. To avoid waterlogging, let any extra water out of the pot freely drain.

- Fertilization

During the growing season, fertilize Phalaenopsis orchids regularly with a balanced fertilizer that has been diluted to half strength. Every two to four weeks, apply fertilizer to encourage healthy growth and flowering.

- Air Circulation

Enable enough ventilation surrounding Phalaenopsis orchids to avert bacterial and fungal infections. Open windows or use oscillating fans to encourage ventilation without exposing the plants to drafts.

Specific Care Requirements

The special maintenance needs of Phalaenopsis orchids set them apart from other orchid species.

- Flower Spike Care

To promote fresh growth and subsequent blooming, cut the flower spike slightly above a node once the blooms have faded. Along the flower spike of certain Phalaenopsis orchids, young plants known as keikis may develop. These plants can be multiplied to generate new plants.

- Humidity Tray

To raise the surrounding humidity, place Phalaenopsis orchids on a humidity tray that is filled with water and pebbles. This is especially useful inside in dry conditions.

- Stake Support

Stakes or trellises can be used to support tall or sprawling flower spikes so they don't break or bend. To bind the spikes without damaging them, use soft ties.

- Reproductive Propagation

It is possible to propagate Phalaenopsis orchids by division, backbulbs, or keikis. You can make new specimens with traits identical to the original plant by dividing adult plants.

- Pest and Disease Management

Regularly check Phalaenopsis orchids for pest indicators, such as mealybugs, aphids, and spider mites. Use neem oil or insecticidal soap to treat infestations as soon as possible. Avoid overwatering and ensure adequate air circulation to prevent bacterial and fungal illnesses.

Chapter 16

Dendrobium and
Cattleya Orchids

Origins and Characteristics

Dendrobium orchids are native to a variety of environments in Asia, Australia, and the Pacific Islands. They are distinguished by their vigorous growth patterns and abundant flowering. They include a vast array of species and hybrids that differ in size, form, and color of the flowers. Typically, dendrobium orchids have cane-like pseudobulbs and erect or arching stems that are covered with clusters of flowers that range in color from white and yellow to purple and magenta.

Cattleya orchids, which are native to Central and South America, are highly valued for their fragrant and enormous, beautiful blooms. They produce pseudobulbs with one or more flowers on top when they grow lithophytically on rocks or epiphytically on trees. Shades of white, pink, purple, and red are just a few of the stunning colors that caterpillar orchids display. They also frequently have contrasting patterns and markings.

Cultivation Techniques

Light and Temperature

- Dendrobium Orchids:

Bright, indirect light is ideal for dendrobium orchid growth. To ensure that they receive enough light without being exposed to direct sunshine, put them close to windows that face either east or west. Maintain temperatures in the range of 65–85°F (18–29°C) during the day and 55–65°F (13–18°C) at night.

- Orchids Cattleya:

Filtered sunshine or brilliant, indirect light is preferred by cattleya orchids. Windowsills facing east or south are the best orientations.

It should be between 70 and 85°F (21 and 29°C) during the day and between 55 and 65°F (13 and 18°C) at night.

Humidity and Air Circulation
- Moderate to high humidity levels are beneficial for both Dendrobium and Cattleya orchids, preferably falling between 50 and 70 percent. Orchids placed on humidity trays with water and pebbles will produce more humidity. To avoid bacterial and fungal infections, there must be sufficient air circulation.

Potting Medium and Repotting
- Orchids of Dendrobium:

Make use of a potting media that drains efficiently, such as sphagnum moss or coarse bark mix. Every two to three years or when the potting medium starts to break down, report Dendrobium orchids.
- Cattleya Orchids:

Cattleya orchids require a potting media that is a little bit stiffer and made of coarse bark mix or a combination of bark and perlite. Every two to three years or when the pseudobulbs outgrow their containers, report Cattleya orchids.

Watering and Fertilization
- Orchids of Dendrobium:

Every seven to ten days, or when the potting medium is completely dry to the touch, give Dendrobium orchids a good watering. During the growing season, apply every 2-4 weeks at half strength of a balanced orchid fertilizer.

- Orchids Cattleya:

Water Cattleya orchids every five to seven days, or when the potting medium is almost dry. During the growing season, fertilize every two to three weeks using a balanced orchid fertilizer that has been diluted to half-strength.

Flower Spike Care

- To encourage new growth and subsequent blooming, remove old flower spikes from Dendrobium and Cattleya orchids once they have finished flowering.

- **Particular Attention Needed**

Dendrobium Orchids:

- Several Dendrobium orchids have a specific dormant season, during which plants need less fertilizer and water. To choose the right care routine, find out the particular needs of your hybrid or species of Dendrobium orchid.

Cattleya Orchids:

- To start blooming, cattleya orchids benefit from a winter hibernation phase marked by less watering and colder temperatures. To keep the plants healthy at this time, provide them with bright, indirect light.

Chapter 17
Oncidium and Dancing Lady Orchids

The origins of oncidium orchids can be found in the varied terrain of Central and South America, where they thrive in the lush jungles and tropical temperatures. There are countless species and hybrids in the large Oncidium genus, and each one has unique characteristics and appeal.

The Dancing Lady orchid embodies the grace and charm of the Oncidium family, fittingly named for its fanciful, dancing-like petals. Oncidium orchids are distinguished by their long, thin pseudobulbs that are decorated with drooping flower sprays. They come in an amazing variety of hues and designs. These blossoms grab the senses with their seductive attractiveness, which is reflected in their vivid hues of yellow, orange, and red as well as their tiny patterns that resemble dancing figures.

Cultivation Techniques

Oncidium and Dancing Lady orchids need careful attention to detail and a delicate balance of environmental conditions to be successfully cultivated. The following methods will help you encourage strong development and colorful blooms in these beautiful orchids.

- **Light and Temperature**

Give your Oncidium orchids lots of bright, indirect light so they may get enough light without being in the direct sun. Windowsills facing east or west provide optimum growth conditions. To replicate their natural habitats, keep daytime temperatures between 65 and 80°F (18 and 27°C) and overnight temperatures between 55 and 65°F (13 and 18°C).

- **Humidity and Air Circulation**

Oncidium orchids require a moderate to high humidity level—ideally between 50 and 70 percent—to thrive. To enhance ambient humidity and guarantee sufficient air circulation to ward against bacterial and fungal infections, use humidity trays loaded with water and pebbles.

- ### *Potting Medium and Repotting*

To encourage strong root growth, choose a potting medium that drains effectively, such as a coarse bark mix or a bark and perlite mixture. Make sure Oncidium orchids have enough room to grow by repotting them every one to two years or when the potting medium starts to break down.

- ### *Watering and Fertilization*

Water Oncidium orchids sparingly, letting the potting media dry up a little in between applications. Make sure to completely submerge the plant with water, but do not overwater as this might cause root rot. During the growing season, fertilize every two to three weeks using a balanced orchid fertilizer that has been diluted to half strength to supply the necessary nutrients for strong development and blooming.

- ### *Flower Spike Care*

Oncidium orchids should have their spent flower spikes trimmed after the bloom cycle to promote fresh growth and further flowering. Certain types of orchids have the potential to yield keikis, or young plants, along the flower spike. This presents a chance for orchid collection growth and propagation.

Particular Attention Needed

- ### *Oncidium Orchids*

Because the Oncidium genus is so diverse, it's important to learn about the particular maintenance needs of the orchid variety you own. Certain Oncidium species may display distinct characteristics or inclinations, requiring customized attention to guarantee their health and vitality.

- ***Dancing Lady Orchids***

Celebrated for their unusual dancing-like flowers, Dancing Lady orchids require similar maintenance to other Oncidium kinds. Observe their light, temperature, humidity, and watering requirements and provide them with the supportive atmosphere they need to thrive.

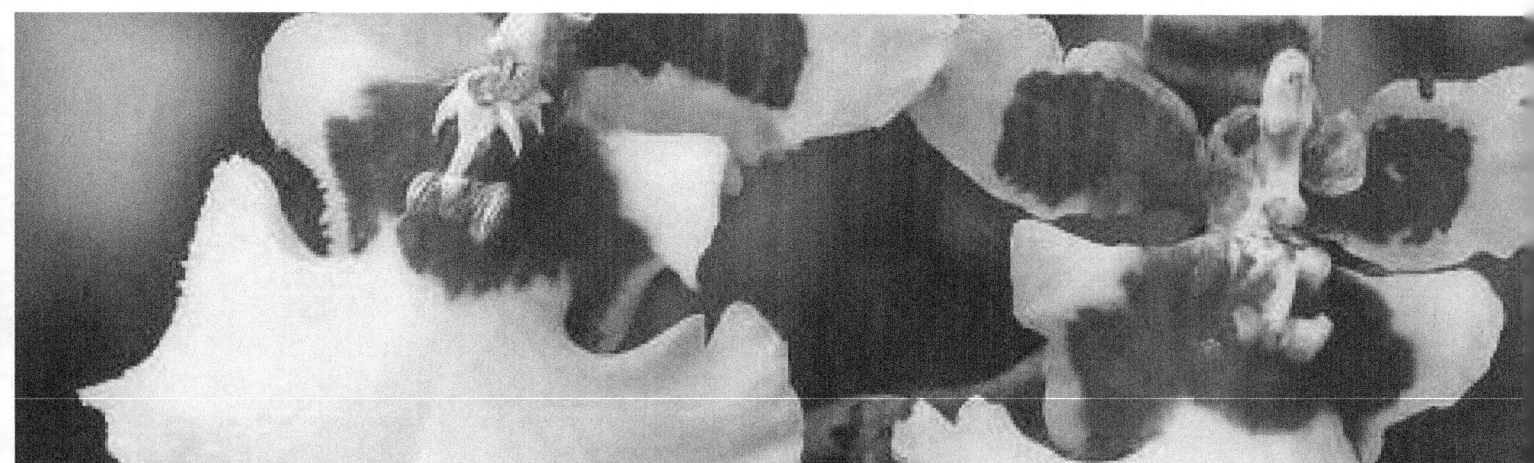

Chapter 18
Vanilla and Other Unique Orchids

Vanilla orchids are highly valued members of the Orchidaceae family, valued for both their unique scent and culinary value.

Origins and Characteristics

- *Vanilla Orchids*

As members of the genus Vanilla, vanilla orchids are native to tropical regions of Central and South America and are the main source of natural vanilla flavoring. These fascinating orchids have clusters of tiny, cream- or pale-green-colored blooms atop long, climbing stalks covered in rich, green leaves. Vanilla orchids are a great addition to any orchid collection because of their culinary and medicinal use in addition to their fragrant flowers.

- *Other Unique Orchids*

Beyond Vanilla orchids, the world of orchids includes a wide range of unusual and remarkable species. Every type of orchid has its unique allure and interest, from the exquisite slipper orchids (Paphiopedilum) with their characteristic pouch-like blooms to the mesmerizing Stanhopea orchids with their elaborate, fragrant petals that grow upside down.

Cultivation Techniques

Vanilla and other unusual orchids require specialized care to fulfill their particular environmental and cultural requirements. You may grow orchids that exhibit their distinct beauty and appeal by adopting the following growing practices and growing healthy, robust plants.

- *Light and Temperature*

Give vanilla orchids bright, indirect light to replicate the understory of a forest, which is their natural home. Windowsills facing east or west provide optimum growth conditions.

To encourage healthy growth and flowering, keep daytime temperatures between 70-85°F (21-29°C) and overnight temperatures between 60-65°F (15-18°C).

Investigate the precise light and temperature needs of other unusual orchids, as these might differ according to the species.

- ***Humidity and Air Circulation***

For Vanilla orchids, create a moist microclimate by setting them on humidity trays that are filled with pebbles and water. For best development and flowering, aim for moderate to high humidity levels between 50–70%. Preventing bacterial and fungal infections requires adequate air circulation, especially in high-humidity settings.

- ***Potting Medium and Repotting***

For Vanilla orchids, use a potting media that drains effectively, such as a coarse bark mix or a bark and perlite mixture. Give vanilla orchids enough room to grow and spread their roots by repotting them every one to two years or when the potting medium starts to break down.

To guarantee that other unusual orchids receive the right care, find out about their preferred potting material and intervals between repottings.

- ***Watering and Fertilization***

When watering Vanilla orchids, use caution and let the potting media dry a little in between applications. Make sure to completely submerge the plant with water, but do not overwater as this might cause root rot.

During the growing season, fertilize every two to three weeks using a balanced orchid fertilizer that has been diluted to half strength to supply the necessary nutrients for strong development and blooming.

Adjust your fertilization and watering schedule for other unusual orchids according to their needs and development patterns.

- **Flower Spike Care**

Vanilla orchids can be encouraged to grow again and bloom again by pruning spent flower spikes after they have finished blossoming. Certain types of orchids have the potential to yield keikis, or young plants, along the flower spike. This presents a chance for orchid collection growth and propagation.

Specific Care Requirements

- **Vanilla Orchids**

For them to flourish and yield vanilla beans, vanilla orchids need a special maintenance schedule. To guarantee effective cultivation and bean production, learn about their unique needs for pollination, pruning, and harvesting.

- **Other Unique Orchids**

Every type of unique orchid may have different needs for maintenance, from certain planting materials to particular fertilizing and watering schedules. To give your orchid species the best care and growing circumstances possible, learn about its specific requirements.

Troubleshooting and Common Issues

Chapter 19
Diagnosing and Treating Common Orchid Problems

Because of their delicate nature and amazing beauty, orchids can be vulnerable to several problems that might impede their development and ability to bloom. To properly care for orchids, ideal circumstances must be provided, as well as rapid and efficient issue diagnosis and treatment.

Yellowing Leaves

For orchid gardeners, yellowing leaves can be a worrisome sight. Numerous factors, such as nutrient shortages, natural aging, overwatering, and underwatering, might contribute to this problem.

The main offender is overwatering, which frequently suffocates the roots and produces yellow leaves. On the other hand, dehydration brought on by underwatering can result in comparable symptoms. Yellowing leaves can also be caused by nutrient deficits, especially those involving nitrogen, or by the aging process itself, which causes older leaves to naturally become yellow and fall off.

The first step in diagnosing yellowing leaves is to measure the moisture content of the potting medium. Examine your fertilization techniques and look for indications of rot or dehydration in the roots. Aeration and moisture should be balanced in your watering schedule. To remedy any nutrient shortages, use a balanced orchid fertilizer, and get rid of really yellowed leaves to stop illness from spreading.

Root Rot

Poor drainage and overwatering are common causes of the dangerous problem known as root rot. Brown or dark, mushy roots that may release an unpleasant stench are usually seen in orchids that have root rot.

Gently remove the orchid from its pot and look at the roots to determine whether it has root rot. Rotted roots are mushy and brown, while healthy roots are strong and white or green.

To cure root rot, remove any impacted roots using sterile scissors and plant the orchid again in recently prepared, well-draining soil. To avoid this happening again, water the pot less frequently and make sure it drains properly.

Leaf Spots and Blotches

Sunburn, bacterial infections, or fungal infections can cause patches and blotches on leaves. Bacterial spots are slimy and wet, while fungal spots are often dry and may have a ring. Brown or black patches on leaves exposed to prolonged direct sunlight are the result of sunburn.

Determine the type of spots and evaluate the plant's exposure to sunlight to determine the reason for leaf spots. Utilize a fungicide to treat fungal diseases and enhance ventilation. Remove the afflicted leaves and use a bactericide to treat bacterial infections. To avoid becoming sunburned during peak hours, adjust the lighting.

Wilting and Drooping Leaves

There are three main causes of wilting and drooping leaves: *root damage, overwatering, and underwatering*. Overwatered orchids have roots that are too wet to properly absorb water, whereas underwatered orchids seem parched. Water intake can also be hampered by physical damage to roots sustained during handling or repotting.

Assessing the moisture content of the potting medium and looking for damage or decay at the roots are two ways to identify withering and drooping leaves.

Before repotting in fresh media, make sure your watering techniques are adjusted to provide adequate hydration and clip any damaged roots.

Failure to Bloom

For growers, it might be disheartening when orchids don't flower. This problem is frequently caused by inadequate light, nutritional imbalances, incorrect temperatures, and insufficient rest intervals.

Determine the orchid's length of exposure and light conditions to determine the root cause of its inability to bloom. Examine the frequency and type of your fertilization and see if you are meeting the orchid's need for a natural rest time.

Gradually increase the amount of sun exposure, apply a greater phosphorus fertilizer to promote blooms, and make sure temperature variations correspond to actual seasonal variations. If your orchids need relaxation time, give them one.

Pest Infestations

Many pests, including aphids, mealybugs, spider mites, and scale, can harm orchids. If these pests are not removed right away, they may cause serious harm.

Regularly check plants for insect indications to diagnose infestations. Seek out tiny insects with a magnifying glass. Use an alcohol-dipped cotton swab to physically remove pests from infestations. Isolate afflicted plants to stop the infection from spreading to other orchids.

Bacterial and Fungal Infections

Common infections such as Pseudomonas, Phytophthora, and Botrytis can result in soft, watery rot, root and crown rot, and gray mold, respectively.

Water splashing, inadequate air circulation, and high humidity are common causes of these diseases.

In addition to smelling the plant for unpleasant odors, look for symptoms like mold, soft rot, and discoloration to diagnose bacterial and fungal illnesses.

To prevent recurrence, treat infections by using sterile equipment to remove diseased areas, administering the proper fungicides or bactericides, and increasing air circulation while lowering humidity levels.

Preventative Measures

Preventive measures must be put in place to reduce the likelihood of common issues when caring for orchids. Watering orchids properly is essential; nevertheless, to prevent waterlogging the roots, let the potting media dry out a little bit in between waterings. Make sure orchids get the proper amount of light for their needs; keep them out of direct sunlight, which can scorch their leaves.

To prevent nutrient deficits or toxicities, balanced fertilization is crucial. Use a balanced fertilizer for orchids and adhere to suggested feeding schedules. To avoid bacterial and fungal infections, keep humidity levels normal and make sure there is adequate air circulation. Keep an eye out for any early warning indicators of issues with orchids so that fast action and treatment can be taken. Reducing the likelihood of disease and pest infestations can also be achieved by keeping the growing environment tidy and debris-free.

Chapter 20

Overcoming Common Growing Challenges

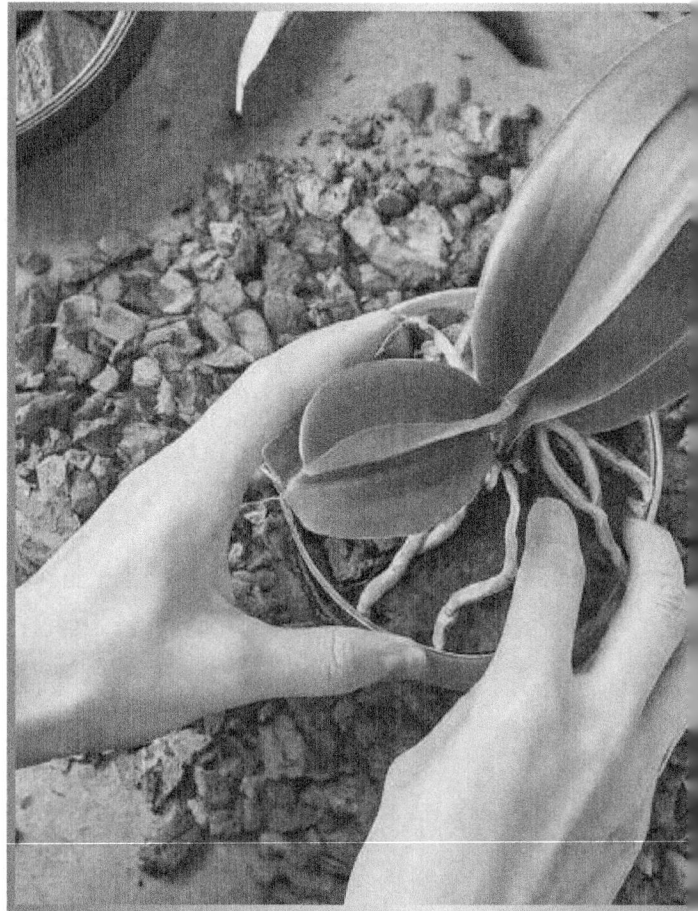

O rchid cultivation is a gratifying yet difficult job. Maintaining vibrant and healthy orchids requires an understanding of and ability to overcome common growing problems. This chapter offers thorough fixes for common problems faced by orchid producers.

1. Light Requirements

- *Challenge:*

Certain orchid species have light needs that, if not satisfied, might result in stunted growth and unflowering.

- *Solution:*

Determine the exact amount of light that your species of orchid needs. Three categories apply to orchids in general: high light, medium light, and low light.

Provide bright, indirect light or filtered sunlight for high-light orchids, including Cattleyas. Oncidiums and other medium-light orchids do best in bright, indirect light, while they can also survive in some shade. Phalaenopsis and other low-light orchids thrive in environments with less light, such as those found indoors away from the sun.

If natural light is insufficient, use grow lights as a supplement. Artificial lights should be placed 6–12 inches above the orchids and left on for 12–16 hours per day. Keep an eye on the color of the leaves; yellowish foliage may suggest too much light, while dark green leaves indicate inadequate light.

2. Variations in Temperature

- *Challenge:*

Because of their sensitivity to temperature fluctuations, orchids can become stressed and struggle to thrive.

- *Solution:*

Keep the temperature consistent for the species of orchids you have. The majority of orchids like temperatures in the range of 70–85°F (21–29°C) during the day and 60–65°F (15–18°C) at night.

Orchids shouldn't be placed next to air conditioners, heating vents, or drafty windows. To keep an eye on temperatures and make any adjustments, use a thermometer. Plants like dendrobiums which depend on seasonal temperature fluctuations to bloom, offer a cooler time of year with less watering.

3. Controlling Humidity

- *Challenge:*

Certain humidity levels are necessary for orchid growth; excessive humidity can encourage fungal infections and cause dehydration.

- *Solution:*

For most orchids, keep humidity levels between 50 and 70 percent. To raise the humidity surrounding the plants, use a humidity tray that is filled with pebbles and water. As you place orchids over the pebbles, make sure the roots are not submerged in water.

Use a humidifier to keep the humidity level appropriate in arid conditions. By using fans to increase air circulation and ensure that the fans do not blow directly over the orchids, fungal illnesses can be avoided.

4. Watering Practices

- *Challenge:*

A typical issue is improper watering, which can result in dehydration or root rot.

- *Solution:*

Give orchids a thorough watering, letting the water run through the potting medium and out of the plant entirely. Once the top inch of the potting material appears dry, water it. Odontals require less water in the cooler months, therefore adjust the frequency according to the climate and season.

If you can, use distilled water or rainwater instead of tap water, as the latter may include minerals that might accumulate in the potting medium.

5. Potting Medium and Repotting

- *Challenge:*

Poor root health might result from using the incorrect potting material or from not repotting frequently enough.

- *Solution:*

Pick a potting medium with adequate aeration and drainage. Sphagnum moss, orchid bark, or a combination of the two are typical options. Orchids should be replanted every 1-2 years or when the potting medium degrades. Repotting avoids compaction and encourages strong root development.

Carefully take the orchid out of its present container, cut off any decaying or dead roots, and then transplant it into new potting soil.

6. Fertilization

- *Challenge:*

Both excessive and insufficient fertilization can have an impact on orchid health.

- *Solution:*

Use half the recommended strength of a balanced, water-soluble fertilizer when fertilizing orchids. During the growing season, fertilizer should be applied every 2-4 weeks. In the dormant season, fertilizer should be reduced or stopped. Once a month, flush the potting media with plain water to avoid fertilizer salt buildup.

7. Pest Control

- *Challenge:*

Many pests, including aphids, mealybugs, spider mites, and scale, can harm orchids.

- *Solution:*

Check orchids frequently for insect activity. By hand, eliminate any visible pests with a cotton swab dipped in rubbing alcohol. Make sure there is no debris and that the growth space is clean. For a few weeks, quarantine newly acquired orchids to avoid bringing pests into your current collection.

8. Disease Management

- *Challenge:*

Orchids are susceptible to fungal and bacterial infections, which can spread swiftly.

- *Solution:*

Make sure there is adequate airflow and don't let the potting medium become too wet. Give orchids a morning watering so that by evening the leaves will have dried. As soon as possible, remove and discard any contaminated plant parts. Apply fungicides to treat fungal infections and bactericides to treat bacterial infections as needed. To stop the spread of illness, sterilize cutting instruments both before and after use.

9. Encouraging Blooming

- *Challenge:*

Many stressors might cause orchids to decline to bloom.

- *Solution:*

Ensure that there is enough light, the optimum temperature, and the right ratio of nutrients. Certain species, including Phalaenopsis, can be stimulated to bloom by a decrease in nighttime temperature. If the orchid needs a rest period, make sure it gets one. Change the fertilization schedule to use a higher phosphorus fertilizer that promotes blooms.

10. Addressing Environmental Stress

- *Challenge:*

Orchids can be shocked by environmental stresses including abrupt changes in temperature, humidity, or light.

- *Solution:*

Acclimate orchids to environmental changes gradually. For instance, begin with a shady spot and progressively increase the amount of light exposure when transferring orchids outdoors for the summer. During transitions, keep a close eye on orchids and make necessary adjustments to minimize stress.

7

Advanced Techniques and Projects

❦

Chapter 21

Creating an Orchid Terrarium

One great approach to growing these exotic plants in a controlled, eye-catching setting is by building an orchid terrarium.

For orchids that need constant attention and high humidity, a terrarium is the perfect environment.

Selecting the Right Container

Selecting a suitable container is the first step in building an orchid terrarium. The container needs to be big enough to support the orchids' growth and have ample airflow. Glass aquariums, big glass jars, or custom-made terrariums are common choices. To facilitate maintenance and simple access, make sure the container has a wide entrance.

It is best to choose a terrarium with a detachable lid so you may adjust the humidity by opening and shutting the lid. If utilizing an aquarium, controlling the airflow while keeping the humidity high can be done with a mesh or glass lid.

Choosing Suitable Orchid Species

Not every kind of orchid can be grown in terrariums. Select orchids that do well in low light and high humidity. Appropriate species consist of:

- Miniature Phalaenopsis: These terrarium-friendly orchids are small and require little maintenance.
- Miniature Cattleyas: These are a little more light-sensitive yet do well in terrarium environments.

Pleurothallids: These orchids, which include genera like Masdevallia and Dracula, like humid, cool climates.

- Jewel Orchids (Ludisia discolor): Prized for their visually appealing leaves and low light needs.

Preparing the Terrarium

- ### *Step 1: Tidy Up the Container*

Use a mild soap and water to give the container a thorough cleaning. This aids in stopping the development of bacteria or mold.

- ### *Step 2: Establish a Drainage Layer*

To avoid waterlogging and root rot, an adequate drainage layer is essential. At the base of the container, start with a layer of coarse gravel or clay pellets. This layer should have a depth of one to two inches.

- ### *Step 3: Including a Shielding Layer*

Cover the drainage layer with a barrier layer, like a piece of landscape fabric or fine mesh. By doing this, the potting medium and drainage material are kept separate.

- ### *Step 4: Add Potting Medium*

Make use of an orchid-friendly potting media that drains properly. It is effective to combine perlite, sphagnum moss, and orchid bark. The material needs to be damp, but not soggy. Cover the barrier layer with a 2 to 3-inch layer of potting medium.

- ### *Step 5: Plant the Orchids*

Shake out any extra potting medium from the roots of the orchids before carefully removing them from their containers. Make sure the orchids have adequate room to grow when you arrange them in the terrarium. For a balanced effect, arrange the taller plants toward the back and the smaller ones near the front. Make sure the roots are firmly secured by covering them with more potting media.

- ***Step 6: Add Decorative Elements***

Add some ornamental items to your terrarium, like driftwood, pebbles, or moss, to make it look better. These enhance the appearance while also aiding in humidity maintenance.

Maintaining the Orchid Terrarium

- ***Watering:***

Watering orchids in a terrarium needs to be done carefully. Because of the enclosed environment's ability to hold moisture, overwatering may cause root rot. Water the orchids in moderation, making sure the potting media stays damp but not drenched. To add humidity to the plants without saturating the medium, lightly sprinkle them with a spray bottle. Watering schedules are determined by the terrarium's environment and the particular requirements of the orchid species.

- ***Humidity:***

Keep the humidity at a high level (60–80%). To check and modify the humidity, use a hygrometer. If the terrarium's humidity falls, spritz the plants more often or add a small dish of water within. On the other hand, partially open the lid to improve airflow if the humidity is too high.

- ***Illumination:***

In a terrarium, orchids require enough indirect light. To prevent the plants from being scorched, place the terrarium next to a bright window rather than in direct sunlight. If there is not enough natural light, utilize grow lights made especially for orchids. Lights should be positioned 6–12 inches above the plants and should be on for 12–14 hours every day.

- ***Climatic temperature:***

Ensure that the temperature range you keep your orchid species in is steady. The majority of orchids like temperatures in the range of 70–80°F (21-27°C) during the day and 60–65°F (15–18°C) at night. To avoid temperature swings, keep the terrarium away from vents that regulate heating or cooling.

- ***Air Movement:***

Enough airflow is essential to stop the formation of mold and fungi. Make sure there is enough airflow in the terrarium by using a small fan or a small gap in the lid. Take care not to produce drafts that could cause the plants to dry up.

- ***Pruning and Grooming:***

To keep your plants looking healthy and attractive, regularly trim away any dead or yellowing leaves and spent flower spikes. To stop the transmission of illness, use sterile pruning shears or scissors. To stop mold from growing, clear the terrarium of any debris.

- ***Fertilization:***

Fertilization is sometimes beneficial for orchids in terrariums. Apply a water-soluble, balanced orchid fertilizer at half the recommended dosage. During the growing season, fertilizer should be applied once a month. Steer clear of overfertilizing because too many nutrients may build up in the small space.

- ***Pest Control:***

Keep a frequent eye out for any indications of pests like mealybugs, spider mites, or aphids in the terrarium. If pests are found, separate the impacted plants and apply neem oil or insecticidal soap to them. To stop infestations, make sure the area is clean and has adequate air circulation.

Chapter 22
Building an Orchid Greenhouse or Conservatory

The construction of an orchid greenhouse or conservatory is a noteworthy undertaking that can offer the ideal conditions for cultivating a varied and flourishing assortment of orchids.

Planning and Design

- ### *Choosing a Location:*

Selecting the ideal site for your greenhouse is essential. To optimize natural light, choose a location that receives plenty of sunlight—ideally with a southern or southeast exposure. Make sure there is adequate drainage in the region to avoid standing water near the foundation. Practicality and ease of use also depend on being close to a water source and power outlets.

- ### *Greenhouse Size:*

Calculate the greenhouse's dimensions based on the quantity and variety of orchids you intend to cultivate. Think about your present collection and your growth plans. Greater control over temperature and humidity as well as greater plant arrangement freedom are provided by larger greenhouses. Make sure the greenhouse's dimensions fit the available area and adhere to any applicable municipal zoning laws.

- ### *Structure Type:*

Choose the kind of greenhouse structure that will work best for you. Freestanding, lean-to, and attached greenhouses are typical choices. The greatest design and placement versatility is provided by freestanding greenhouses, but they do need more room. Attached and lean-to greenhouses are great for limited locations since they are economical and use the support of existing structures.

- ### *Materials:*

Choose sturdy materials to build the greenhouse with. Wood, aluminum, and galvanized steel are typical materials.

Aluminum is low maintenance, lightweight, and resistant to rust. Although heavier, galvanized steel is robust and long-lasting. Although wood has a natural appearance, it needs greater upkeep to avoid rot and insect damage. Pick a material that strikes a balance between price, toughness, and aesthetics.

- *Glazing:*

The glazing material has an impact on durability, insulation, and light transmission. Glass, polycarbonate, and polyethylene film are among the options. Although glass is long-lasting and has good light transmission, it is heavy and costly. Although polycarbonate is more expensive than polyethylene, it is lightweight, strong, and offers good insulation. The least expensive choice is polyethylene film, but it needs to be changed frequently. If you live in an area where there are large temperature changes, you may want to look into double or triple-glazing for improved insulation.

Construction

- *Basis:*

A strong base is necessary for the greenhouse to be stable and long-lasting. Treated wood, concrete footings, and concrete slabs are common forms of foundations. Make sure the foundation is level and that water is sufficiently drained from the building. A concrete slab is suggested for a permanent structure due to its solidity and longevity.

- *Frame Construction:*

Assemble the greenhouse frame according to your design plans or the manufacturer's instructions. To guarantee the integrity of the structure, use connectors and fasteners that are resistant to corrosion. To endure wind and weather, make sure all joints are well attached. Make sure that the structure is sound regularly and tighten any loose fasteners.

- *Glazing Installation:*

To stop leaks and drafts, properly install the glazing material. Use the appropriate sealing materials and processes for panels made of glass and polycarbonate. Make sure there are no gaps and that all of the panels are firmly attached. When using polyethylene film, make sure it is stretched securely over the frame and fastened firmly with clips or battens. Check the glazing frequently for damage, and replace any worn-out or damaged sections.

- *Ventilation:*

Controlling humidity and temperature requires proper ventilation. To promote air circulation, install louvered windows, side vents, and roof vents. To ensure consistent ventilation without the need for user intervention, think about utilizing automated vent openers that react to temperature fluctuations. If required, add fans to natural ventilation to enhance air circulation and avoid stagnant air pockets.

- *Doors and Pathways:*

Install doors that let light through while preserving the insulating qualities of the greenhouse. Good choices include weatherstripping on hinged doors or sliding doors. Use materials like gravel, concrete, or paving stones for durability and drainage when designing paths, making sure they are wide enough for pleasant travel and maintenance tasks. To avoid mishaps, make sure all walkways have a non-slip surface and are level.

Climate Control

- *Heating:*

For optimal growth, orchids need constant temperatures. To maintain ideal temperatures during the winter, install a heating system.

Radiant floor heating, propane heaters, and electric heaters are available options. Make sure the temperature stays within the optimal range for your species of orchid by using thermostats to control it. Make sure the greenhouse's heating system is the right size, and think about adding backup power sources in case of crises.

- ***Cooling:***

Invest in a cooling system to avoid overheating throughout the summer. Fans for ventilation, evaporative coolers, and shade cloths are available options. While evaporative coolers use water evaporation to effectively chill spaces, shade cloths can also help prevent solar heat absorption. Put in ventilation fans to improve airflow and lessen temperature fluctuations. To keep the environment steady, keep a close eye on temperatures and make necessary adjustments to cooling techniques.

- ***Humidity Control:***

Keep the high humidity levels necessary for the growth of orchids. To raise humidity, use misting systems, humidifiers, or wet walls. Install a hygrometer to track humidity levels and make necessary adjustments. In addition to maintaining a balanced humidity, proper ventilation also inhibits the growth of bacteria and fungi. To avoid mold and mildew, regularly clean and maintain humidity equipment.

Manual Watering:

- ***Manual Watering:***

Smaller greenhouses can be adequately watered by hand using hoses or watering cans. To prevent mineral buildup from tap water, use distilled water or rainfall. Give orchids a good watering, letting the water run off the pots. Maintain a regular watering schedule and make adjustments in response to plant requirements and seasonal variations.

- *Automated Watering Systems:*

Take into account automatic watering methods, such as misting or drip irrigation, for larger greenhouses. Water is delivered to the roots using drip irrigation, which minimizes waste and guarantees uniform dispersal. Misting systems are perfect for orchids that need high humidity because they offer steady humidity levels and gentle watering. To guarantee correct operation and prevent waterlogging or underwatering, do routine maintenance and inspections on the automated systems.

Lighting

- *Natural Light:*

Arrange the greenhouse to receive as much sunshine as possible to maximize natural light. Regular cleaning of the glazing will guarantee optimal light transmission. During the hours of maximum sunshine, use shading materials such as whitewash or shade cloths to filter light and avoid scorching. To ensure that orchids receive the right amount of light, regularly modify the shading in response to seasonal variations in light.

- *Supplemental Lighting:*

Add artificial grow lights as a complement in regions with low natural light. Energy-efficient LED grow lights offer the complete spectrum of light required for orchid growth. Place the lights so that they evenly distribute light around the greenhouse. Set timers to automatically adjust lighting to replicate the cycles of natural daylight.

Shelving and Benching

- *Shelving:*

Put in place robust shelf units to accommodate orchid pots. For durability, use materials like treated wood or galvanized steel.

Make sure the shelves can be adjusted to fit different-sized and developmental orchids. Plants should be arranged to provide enough sun exposure and air circulation without being crowded.

- *Benching:*

Establish benching systems for specimen plants and larger orchids. For pleasant upkeep, benches should be waist-high and feature slatted surfaces to let air flow around the pots. Make use of materials that won't rot or absorb moisture. If you want to move and rearrange benches easily, think about putting benches on wheels.

Maintenance and Care

- *Regular Monitoring:*

Regularly check the temperature, humidity, and light levels in the greenhouse. To maintain ideal conditions, make necessary adjustments to climate control systems. Regularly check orchids for disease or insect activity. Maintain thorough records of the plant's health and environmental circumstances so that you can see trends and make wise decisions.

- *Sanitation and Cleaning:*

To stop the spread of illness and pests, keep the greenhouse clean. Clear away fallen flowers, dead leaves, and trash right away. Regularly use a moderate bleach solution or other horticultural disinfectants to clean benches, shelves, and tools. To keep your orchids in a healthy environment, schedule routine deep cleanings.

- *Control of Pests:*

Use integrated pest management (IPM) techniques to keep pests under control. To control pest populations, introduce beneficial insects like ladybugs and predatory mites. As directed on the label, apply horticultural oils and insecticidal soaps as needed.

Keep an eye out for pests on your plants and act quickly to stop infestations from getting worse.

Seasonal Modifications

- *Winter:*

Make sure the heating system is operating properly to keep the temperature comfortable. As orchid development slows, watering frequency should be reduced. To make up for the decreased daylight hours, use grow lights. Keep an eye on humidity levels and adjust humidifiers as necessary to keep orchids from suffering from dry air.

- *Summer:*

To avoid overheating, utilize shade materials and increase ventilation. As the growth rate of orchids rises, water them more frequently. Keep an eye on the humidity levels and adjust misting systems and humidifiers as necessary. Keep an eye out for symptoms of heat stress and act quickly to address them.

Expanding and Upgrading

Your greenhouse may need to be upgraded or expanded as your collection of orchids increases. Make room for future projects by leaving space surrounding the greenhouse in case it grows. To accommodate more orchids, think about putting in automated climate control systems, sophisticated lighting arrangements, or extra shelves and benching. To maximize growing conditions, evaluate the greenhouse's functioning regularly and make any modifications.

Chapter 23

Hybridizing and Creating New Orchid Varieties

Creating attractive and distinctive new orchid types through hybridization is an exciting and fulfilling effort. Gaining proficiency in these methods will enable you to appreciate the creative challenge of creating your distinctive plants while also adding to the vast diversity of orchid species.

Understanding Orchid Genetics

- ***Basic Principles:***

To create offspring with traits from both parents, two distinct orchid species or hybrids are crossed in a process known as orchid hybridization. Genes that control characteristics including bloom color, shape, size, and scent are encoded in each orchid's DNA. You can affect the qualities of the progeny by choosing parent plants with desired attributes.

- ***Dominant and Recessive Traits:***

In orchids, traits can be recessive or dominant. Recessive features could remain hidden unless both parent plants contain the recessive gene, whereas dominant qualities are more likely to manifest in the progeny. It is easier to forecast the results of your hybridization efforts when you are aware of the interactions between these qualities.

- ***Generational Breeding:***

To establish desirable features, orchid hybridization frequently requires breeding across several generations. To fine-tune and fix the traits in later generations (F2, F3, etc.), selective breeding must be continued. The first-generation (F1) hybrids may exhibit a wide variety of characteristics.

Selecting Parent Plants

- ***Desirable Traits:***

Select parent plants according to which specific features you want to combine or improve. Color, size, form, scent, blooming season, and plant vigor are a few examples of these characteristics. Plants that exhibit robust health and a robust floral history are prime candidates for hybridization.

- ***Compatibility:***

Make sure the parent plants you have chosen are suitable for breeding. Although it is possible to cross most orchids within the same genus, intergeneric hybrids—that is, crossings between distinct genera—are more difficult and may call for specific methods. Examine whether the species or hybrids you intend to cross are compatible.

- ***Health and Vigor:***

To improve the odds of a successful hybridization, choose parent plants that are disease-free and in good condition. Plants that are robust and vigorous have a higher probability of yielding seeds and healthy progeny.

Pollination Process

- ***Pollinia Extraction:***

Pollinia, or compact clumps of pollen, are present inside orchid flowers. You must first remove the pollinia from the selected male parent flower to hybridize orchids. To avoid damaging the flower, carefully remove the pollinia using tweezers or a sterilized toothpick.

- ***Pollination:***

Place the pollinia on the selected female parent flower's stigma. The stigma is situated at the apex of the column, frequently close to the lip's base of the flower.

To ensure proper pollination, set the pollinia on the stigma with care, making sure to make good contact. To ensure accurate records, label the pollinated bloom with the date and information about the parent plant.

- **Post-Pollination Care:**

Following pollination, a seed pod will form and the fertilized bloom will start to wither. Depending on the species, orchid seed pods may take many months to mature. Provide the best growing circumstances possible at this time, with steady temperatures, high humidity, and adequate light.

Seed Pod Harvesting and Sterilization

- **Pod Development:**

Observe the developing seed pod. As the pod ripens, its texture and color will alter. To prevent losing the seeds, harvest the pod when it is fully developed but before it cracks apart. Research the particular requirements of your orchid species as maturation times vary.

- **Sterilization:**

Because they are so tiny, orchid seeds are easily contaminated. The seed pod and seeds should be sterilized to guarantee proper germination. To start, wash the seed pod with a moderate bleach solution (1:10 bleach to water) to get rid of any surface impurities. Rinse the pod well with sterile water after sterilization.

Seed Sowing Techniques

- **In Vitro Germination:**

Usually, orchid seeds are planted in vitro—that is, on a nutrient-rich media in a sterile laboratory setting. The greatest possibility of germination and robust growth is offered by this technique.

To prevent contamination, set up a sterile work area and utilize sterile instruments and containers.

- **Preparation of Nutrient Medium:**

Get ready a nutritional medium that will help the seeds of orchids germinate. Typically, the medium comprises carbohydrates, minerals, vitamins, and agar. Transfer the ready media into sterile Petri dishes or culture flasks and let it set.

- **Sowing Seeds:**

Crack open the sterilized seed pod and gently drop the seeds over the nutritional media while maintaining sterility. To prevent crowding, make sure the seeds are distributed evenly. Label the containers with the date and the information about the parent plant after sealing them.

Germination and Seedling Care

- **Germination:**

The seeded containers should be kept in a warm, well-lit area. Keep the temperature steady (around 77°F, or 25°C) and the humidity high. Several weeks to several months may pass before germination occurs, depending on the species of orchid.

- **Seedling Development:**

Protocorms, which are tiny, undifferentiated structures, emerge early in the seedling stage when leaves start to show, and in later stages when roots begin to take shape. Sustain ideal growing circumstances and keep an eye out for contaminants.

- **Transplanting:**

The seedlings must be moved to bigger containers with the new nutrient medium as soon as they are big enough to handle. Replating is the process of creating more room and nutrients for further growth. Treat seedlings cautiously to prevent injury.

Acclimatization and Hardening Off

- *Acclimatization:*

The seedlings will be prepared for acclimatization to regular growing settings following many months of in vitro growth. Expose the seedlings to increasing amounts of light and decreasing humidity gradually. To begin with, set them up in a humid, darkened space, such as a greenhouse or terrarium.

- *Hardening Off:*

The seedlings can be moved to individual pots with an appropriate orchid potting mixture once they have adjusted. Maintain a high humidity level and progressively lower it over time. During this phase of transition, keep a vigilant eye out for any indications of disease or stress in the seedlings.

Growing and Blooming

- *Stages of Growth:*

Before maturing, hybrid orchids will go through some growth stages. To promote healthy growth, give the best possible care, such as the right amount of light, fertilizer, and watering. Hybrids might take several years to achieve blooming size, so be patient.

- *Primary Bloom:*

A hybrid orchid's first bloom is a momentous occasion. It offers the first look at the special qualities of the new hybrid. Keep track of the bloom and assess the effectiveness of your hybridization attempts by contrasting it with the parent plants.

- *Selection and Assessment:*

Consider the hybrid in light of your initial breeding objectives. Examine the size, form, color, scent, and general vigor of the plant in the flowers.

Choose the best individuals to be bred or propagated further. Less desirable plants should be discarded or used for other experimental crosses.

Record Keeping and Documentation

- **Detailed Records:**

Keep thorough records of every hybridization attempt, including information on the parent plants, dates of pollination, the maturation of the seed pods, and the growth of the seedlings. Precise documentation facilitates monitoring advancements, assesses results, and steers future breeding decisions.

- **Photography:**

Take pictures of each step of the hybridization process. Visual records aid in illuminating the traits and growth of your hybrids and offer invaluable points of reference.

- **Labeling:**

Provide pertinent information, such as hybrid identification numbers, pollination dates, and parent plant names, on all plants, seed pods, and containers. Accurate record-keeping is ensured and confusion is avoided with consistent labeling.

Conclusion

Finally it is important to take stock of all we have accomplished as a team. This book delves deep into orchid cultivation, covering everything from the beginnings to advanced techniques, to become a comprehensive resource for orchid enthusiasts at all levels.

- ***A Review of the Trip***

We started by learning about orchids, their function, and the characteristics that set them apart from other interesting plants. To better understand the enduring fascination with orchids among humans, we dove into their cultural importance and long history of beauty.

Species, hybrids, and growth patterns of orchids (including lithophytes, epiphytes, and terrestrial orchids) were all covered in Part 1. This groundwork for understanding laid the groundwork for delving into the intricacy and variety of orchid culture.

In Part 2, we covered the basics of orchid care, including how to choose the best plants for beginners, how to set up your growing area, and how to repot. Anyone new to orchid farming will find these chapters to be an excellent starting point.

Orchid care principles were covered in Part 3, where we reviewed the critical requirements for lighting, humidity, watering, fertilizers, and trimming. These chapters armed you with the skills to care for your orchids and ensure their healthy growth.

In Part 4, we went into advanced orchid care, including temperature control, pest and disease management, and the nuances of growing and cross-breeding orchids. These chapters gave you the knowledge to tackle more tough parts of orchid growing and take your talents to the next level.

Part 5 focuses on specific orchid care for different popular species, such as Phalaenopsis, Dendrobium, Cattleya, Oncidium, and Vanilla orchids. These chapters offered specialized recommendations for each species, guaranteeing that you can provide the finest care for your favorite orchids.

Troubleshooting and common issues were addressed in Part 6, helping you diagnose and treat common problems, and overcome expanding challenges. This section intends to equip you to face any issues you might meet on your orchid gardening adventure.

Finally, Part 7 featured advanced techniques and tasks, including producing orchid terrariums, erecting greenhouses or conservatories, and hybridizing orchids. These chapters sparked imagination and ingenuity, pushing you to experiment and broaden your orchid-growing pursuits.

- ***The Journey Ahead***

Orchid cultivation is a lifetime journey of learning and discovery. The knowledge and abilities you have received from this tutorial are just the beginning. As you continue to nurture and care for your orchids, remember that patience, observation, and a willingness to experiment are crucial to success.

Whether you are a beginner taking your first steps or an expert trying to develop your techniques, this guide has sought to be a beneficial companion. The world of orchids is wide and full of wonder, and there is always more to discover and explore.

- ***Final Thoughts***

I hope that "Orchids Plant Care Guide" has provided you with the inspiration, knowledge, and confidence to pursue your passion for orchids. May your orchid farming journey be full of beauty, progress, and infinite interest.

Printed in Dunstable, United Kingdom